REAL ESTATE MONEY

"How To Make Money From Real Estate"

By

Dave Grandone

TABLE OF CONTENTS

INTRODUCTION

A re you fresh to investing in real estate? Knowing how to invest in real estate doesn't have to be complex, complicated or costly. In this book, you'll learn how to start investing in real estate from start to finish — with no marketing, false claims or pitches.

The book was published to familiarize us with the most current and widely encountered papers, terminology and levels of return correlated with investing in real estate.

With the housing market, particularly in recent years, continuing to improve, more Americans are becoming willing to take part in investing in real estate. Although this could be an appealing concept for others, it is important to consider what investing in real estate is, and what sort of investment one may create. One can learn the fundamentals in only a couple of hours, and spend a lifetime attempting to understand all the complexities, a few brief explanations to act as introductions are below.

There's no better way to get started when you're thinking about investing in real estate than educating yourself. The earlier you learn, the easier the result of the scenario would be as you move into the scenario. Knowledge is strength and, in the real estate universe, strength in your pocket can be transformed into capital. The more experience you have of the real estate environment, the better part you'll be. Through understanding all of the field's dimensions, you should be prepared to take advantage of the investment opportunity that could come your way.

Perhaps, real estate investing classes are delivered in a few various places around you, and you don't even realize this. Visit with your community college to see if they are providing an ongoing training course on the subject when they don't actually give one call around to the companies in your region to inquire whether they will still be offering investment courses. When they don't answer you to inquire when they know anyone they do. Switch to your machine when you have come up with nothing. The Web gives you loads of alternatives to the usual path in classroom spending. You will check for content, discover ideas, and occasionally even chat live with someone who's been a big success in the real estate business and who wants to discuss it.

Real estate is a sector which is innovative and seductive. Totalling today a multi-trillion - dollar industry, real estate is continuing to expand and is a critical part of existence. In short, we all see the need for roofs over our heads, be it in our homes, in the workplace, when engaging in leisure activities, etc., and these roofs are built with certain materials and a specific purpose. Important considerations in recognizing the real estate business industry structure are rooted in the following concepts: finance, risk and expenditure.

Conceptually investment in real property is easy. The goal is to bring capital in, cause it to grow, and there will be much more investment available in the future. Although a degree of risk is needed for any transactions, the expected benefit must exceed the sum of risk involved. Take, for example, the Monopoly game. To win, one buys a property, avoids bankruptcy and collects rent to help provide even more property. If only this were so fast! The principle is very common in life, but an error in the investing cycle can have significant implications.

Real estate accounts for 60 per cent of the conventional assets in the world—and a large portion of all global, business, and personal property. With that in mind, investment in real estate obviously merits respect from any person or company searching for asset groups in which a portion of their money may be allocated.

But before you can make good decisions on whether to invest in real estate or not and which of the many forms of real estate could make the most sense for you, you need to learn the fundamentals of investing in real estate first.

WHAT IS REAL ESTATE?

The word "real estate" applies to property and everything that is connected to that ground. Real estate is sometimes termed real assets.

Lots of people think of property, or houses, or certain forms of buildings and structures when they hear the word real estate. Those are real estate elements but far from being a full concept.

Real estate is the property and everything, such as homes, vehicles, fences and plants, is permanently connected to it. Real estate is also called immovable property.

What qualifies as "permanently attached" to the immovable property also depends on local, state, and federal laws and what was specifically cited in a land sales contract. Property and immovable property are not like personal property.

Personal property refers to immovable property. Appliances such as washers and dryers can be purchased or sold with a house, but are not considered a part of the land. Likewise, the title to underland resources can be sold separately from the land itself. Whether you are attached to the owner's appliances in stainless steel or want to mine for gold in your new backyard, it is crucial to include those information in writing while purchasing or selling real estate.

This is how the Uniform Standards of Qualified Appraisal Practice (USPAP), the industry guide for real estate appraisers, identifies immovable property: "Defined parcel or tract of land, including improvements, if any." This relation to improvements is essential to your definition of immovable property because it stresses that immovable property often encompasses everything stable or permanently connected.

Improvements, as interpreted in the real estate sense, may include a house, restaurant, office building, or some other form of land-built structure. But it can also apply to anything else that is permanently attached to that area, including walls, paths, lakes, trees and even the land utilities. Finally, the immovable property can also include some privileges found in a piece of property — such as air rights, water rights and mineral rights to any natural resources on the earth under the land.

What Is A Real Estate Investor?

With that all-inclusive definition of real estate in opinion, we can now define a real estate investor as an individual (or business or other entity) who invests in the real estate market by buying, leasing or otherwise attaining rights to a real estate property or any of the rights inherent in a piece of real estate.

Of this reason, we explained in the introduction that there are too many forms of investment in real estate. Investing in real estate mostly consists of certain types of assets that most people think about instantly when they hear the term — like purchasing a residential or commercial property and renting out such property, or buying those properties to upgrade easily and resell for income. But it may also apply to a variety of other investment possibilities, like owning and then selling mining rights to a piece of property, or engaging in an investment trust in real estate. And now, real estate investing may also include actively engaging in a big deal through a crowdfunding site for the property.

What Are The Types Of Real Estate?

There are three main types of traditional, physical real estate.

1. **Residential real estate**: It applies to a property where visitors will live or work, like single-family residences, houses, resorts, and holiday homes. Residential real estate owners earn money by receiving rent from renters or selling a home that has risen in value.

2. **Commercial real estate:** It is a structure or land — consider shopping malls, factories, and industrial complexes — where a business is conducted. Commercial real estate may involve manufacturing properties (where products are made and stored, such as factories) and retail property (where goods or services are offered, such as malls). Commercial property owners often make money by collecting rent from tenants and by increasing the future valuation of the property, which generates income when sold.

3. **Raw land:** This can be bought and sold as is, or developed. It can be difficult to invest in a new land and brings more risk than investing in established buildings. Raw land still has no means of producing income until you develop on it, hire it or use it for agricultural purposes.

INVESTING IN REAL ESTATE

If you own a home, you have already invested in real estate, and if you enjoy taking care of the land, you may suggest buying and renting more conventional properties. Even if you don't want to be a landlord, you can add properties to your portfolio instead.

One way is through publicly-traded REITs or trusts in real estate investments. REITs are industries that own and sometimes operate real estate generating income. Every year, REITs are expected to refund at least 90 per cent of their taxable profits to owners, making them a common option among those receiving daily income distributions — called dividends — from their investment.

Publicly traded REITs provide strong liquidity rates (meaning you can quickly purchase and sell them) since their securities are listed on stock markets.

One non-traditional investing choice for real estate is to invest in a crowdfunding site for immobilities. Many of these nontraded or private REITS offerings tend to be less liquid than publicly-traded REITs. These sites, in exchange, tend to deliver a high rate of return.

What Is Real Estate Investing?

In general, investing in real estate is the purchase, holding, renting or sale of land or buildings for the overall purpose of earning income. Investments may concentrate on a property in residential, commercial or industrial real estate.

Residential properties apply to single-family houses, townhomes and condominiums while industrial properties relate to a company house. Examples of a commercial property involve hotels, shops, or clusters of residences, depending on the number of occupants each apartment may contain. Eventually, industrial properties, like distribution or manufacturing facilities or power stations, are assets that are used for industrial uses. Keeping in mind the various forms of properties, what are some of the approaches developers may use to earn money from the real estate industry?

Interest From Loans

Investors have the choice of focusing on credits to raise profits. In the case, a lender is bringing together a loan for a developer of real estate. As with credit cards, developers would be liable for paying interest each month on their loan. The interest charges that the investors are liable for in this case are part of how an investor earns money. In the unfortunate event where a deal goes bad, noteholders (lenders) are paid back before equity holders (investors), thereby offering the lender less risk.

Appreciation

Only real estate owners can earn money by land appreciation. In this approach, buyers would purchase a property they believe will add value. When they see an increase in the value of the property, also known as an appreciation, they can profit as a consequence of the value increase. Unlike loan interest which usually provides smaller yet stable compensation to investors, appreciations provide a large one-time payoff to the investor. It is a common choice for experienced buyers because they appreciate the diligence required to identify a purchasing property that has the potential to maximize valuation.

Lease

Investors do have the right to rent it out after they purchase a house. Under this case, homeowners earn money by making renters live on the property and charging rental rates under return for staying there each month. It is a standard procedure with both private and commercial buildings throughout the United States. Investors who rent out their properties to the general population may handle the tenants themselves, and some prefer to hire a property maintenance firm to deal maintain the land itself. Normally, one will like their rent to cover both costs and liabilities for property with an extra spread or the water.

Investing in real estate can be a difficult business to join so understanding the various options available will help new buyers gain a better understanding of how to make money. Real estate investing will only continue to grow as the valuation of the property in cities across the United States continues to rise.

What Are The Potential Benefits Of Real Estate Investing?

Although no type of investment can offer a profit guarantee or even safety of the principal, for centuries real estate has been one of the best asset classes for investors while at the same time offering gain potential.

Investing in real estate generally offers some possible benefits not associated with other types of investments. Below are just two of those benefits.

Leverage

One of the most important incentives provided by real estate investors is their opportunity to maximize their investments many times over. In other terms, real estate investors can use lent funds to invest in a piece of real estate that they couldn't afford to buy directly, but then know all the potential profit from that property's possession. However, it is also important to point out that increased risk comes with increased leverage.

Tax Benefits

Real estate can provide various types of tax benefits, too. The law, for example, recognizes real estate earnings as capital gains and are paid lower than income from jobs. In fact, the tax base of your investment assets will decrease over time, as the tax system requires you to depreciate your property every year. Often, if you produce cash income from a rented home, you might theoretically reap such earnings free of taxes on self-employment.

Control

The enhanced influence they have over their assets is another dimension of real estate investing that certain people consider beneficial. When you purchase securities or mutual funds, otherwise you actually have to wait passively for certain investments to increase in value. Unless you're a major shareholder in those firms, you 're not going to have an influence over their affairs, which often implies that you can't do anything to improve the value of your assets significantly. Nevertheless, when investing in real estate, you will have some leverage over virtually any variable — acquiring expertise or bargaining abilities to obtain a reasonable price on the transaction, upgrading the land, discovering innovative ways to produce additional income (for example, introducing washing machines to your apartment complex), etc.

There are also many possible advantages of investing in real estate — it will shield your money against depreciation, have tax write-offs on your other profits, etc.

Real Estate Investing Risks

Clearly, no real estate investment debate will be complete without also addressing the risks involved. Immobilier bears the possibility of failure as in any company. In the case of deliberately investing in real estates, such as owning a rental home to rent out, you bear the continuing possibility of vacancy, which can result in a loss of revenue on that land, as well as a downturn in the real estate sector, which will decrease the investment value.

There are also dangers inherent with passive real estate investments — such as holding equity of real estate-related companies, owning securities of real estate investment trusts (REITs), or engaging with real estate transactions by crowdfunding sites, both of which we will explore below. The valuation of such assets may decrease over time in the case of such investments. For these purposes, both passive and active real estate investments will demand you to do your own proper checks and research in advance, just as any other type of investment would require you to.

What Are Real Estate Investing Companies?

We spoke about individual real estate owners up until this stage, but a large portion of all real estate is purchased and operated by real estate investment companies. They are typically grouped as conventional enterprises — corporations, LLCs, LLPs, etc.

Real estate investment funds are primarily equity organizations who collect money from other creditors and use the money to purchase real estate, either for long-term cash flow and growth or for short-term recovery and income.

Large businesses engage in real estate in almost the same manner that private individuals do — but the bigger and more experienced corporations typically participate in transactions that are much greater or more complicated than a single real estate buyer might afford. Many of the larger real estate investment companies also purchase land and then grow the properties themselves — apartment complexes, shopping malls.

But after creating the business (for legal and tax purposes), raising money and then seeking the best real estate opportunities are the only prerequisites for operating a real estate investment firm, this can be achieved by private owners.

Tips for Getting Started in Real Estate Investing

If you're going to succeed in anything in life, including investing in real estate, you've got to want to do it. As for something that brings pleasure or enjoyment, desire is described as longing. Desire emphasizes feeling strength and often implies a strong intention or goal. If you don't want to learn and grow as a human being and really get pleasure from it in real estate investment, then real estate investment will be hard to do. It gives me a lot of pleasure when I go out and look at a house. Each aspect gives me the pleasure of talking to buyers, working out how to make a contract, buying the house, and finding a good homeowner or tenant for the house. Investing in real estate may not be for everyone, but investing in real estate can give anyone the financial freedom that we all want. If you don't want to invest property that's cool, it can still help you live your dreams and help you get to where you want to go in the future.

Why does real estate spend an excellent avenue to fulfil all their dreams?

Let me ask you a couple of questions. Have you got enough money to do whatever you want?

Have you got anything you want? Any debt at all? A lovely house? Good wedding? The right to do anything, no matter how much it costs and how long it takes? If you've got all this stuff, then you're one of the few people that do it in America. Many people can work 50 hours a week and make enough to pay their bills. Most people in today's day and age are living paycheck to paycheck never really knowing if they are going to make enough to pay the bills that just keep piling up. If you are unable to keep up with your monthly bills, how do you plan to retire or send your children to college or have time to enjoy life? It is becoming financially free to answer all these questions. Now it won't be easy for everyone to get off the sofa and get out of their comfort zone. Real estate has proven to be one of the fastest ways to start living the life you deserve. Everybody wants something else out of their lives. Others dream of travelling around the world, spending more time with friends, volunteering, golfing, relaxing on a beach, giving back to the community, or anything to make them happy again. Thousands of things make people happy.

It takes a person who has a deep desire to change their life for the better and think big to make it in real estate. Anyone can be a great investor in real estate. It's going to take a lot of effort. The people who make it into investing in real estate all have a few things in common. Next, like any other company out there, they run their real estate investment business. First, they're going out there and interacting with everyone. Many people can be like me and have difficult conversations with others. If you're all right, anyone can learn how to become a citizen of the community, it just takes a lot of hard work every day. You've got to push beyond your comfort zone. The third thing is you can't be afraid of failing. Everyone has suffered, but the most successful people have learned their lessons from their failures. The fourth thing is you've got to put together a good squad. In a later chapter, I'm going to put a team together. The concept of putting together a team is to have team members that know what to do and can assist you in answering questions when you don't know anything. They can also make sure you don't work to death on your own. You don't want to be the guy in your company doing everything. Doing all is a loss receipt. You must put good people together on whom you can trust and rely. The third thing you need is to have a mentor. The urge to do it is the sixth and last. If they don't want to do it and don't get satisfaction from what they're doing, nobody can be good at something.

One of the most important aspects of achieving what you want in life is setting goals and writing them down.

How are you going to start writing down your goals?

You should think big first, and I mean HUGE by big. If your ambitions are too low, you can achieve them quickly and have nothing else to look forward to. If I had all the money and time in the world what I would do, what I would buy, how I would spend my time, and how I would spend my energy, you would start by asking yourself the question. Starting to write down these? You ought to be well. Think about what you want, spend time with your family, travel the world, the best cars, a house, own a small country, run for president, have the largest real estate investment company in your region or country. Write it down whatever your desires and whatever you want from your life. Some of my aspirations are getting free, going around the world, driving a Porsche, having 10-holiday homes around the world. Right now I'm just trying to get you out of your thought comfort zone and let your imagination runoff.

There are a number of ways of setting goals. I've learned a lot of ways you can set goals, and there's no way you can set goals. The best way I've found to set the goals is to split them into two groups. First, your goals for the short term. This should be goals ranging from a month to about a year. The second is your long-term goals. You think these goals are great goals and what you see for your future.

For the first year, I like to make a list of what I want to do this year, and I'm going to give you an example of how to do it. For the first year, you want to be very precise; first, you want to mention what you want your salary to be at the end of the year, then how much cash you want in the bank (this is money in your account, not assets). First, you'd like to mention how much you'll give. Giving is a very important thing, it can be giving charity, giving friends and family gifts, giving your school or anything you can dream of. So long as it brings joy to others who need it more than you do. First, mention what bad habits you're going to get rid of. Weather is quitting smoking, spending too much on junk, drinking too much, working too much, spending too little time with family, spending too much television, not exercising and much more. We all have bad habits to change in order to evolve as human beings. List several steps under each of these bad habits that you can take to leave them. If you're in a bad habit, you're lazy, and you don't work out enough to improve that. Okay, you can get a gym membership or a plan for home workouts. Commit yourself to follow a plan to work 3-5 days a week. You have to be fully committed and follow through with a detailed plan you set for yourself to change these bad habits. You will start listing some items you want to achieve or do in the next year after you have your plans in place. This can be a successful business start-up, spending time with family, travelling to 2-5 locations, etc. You should now write a detailed plan under each of these about what you need to do and what you need to do to achieve these goals. Finally, you should take all this knowledge that you've got a page-writing about what you see your next year's life being. Goals: Year One That's what I'm going to do this year's income: $500,000 Cash: $100,000 Give $20,000 Bad Habits that are going to change: Sleeping 1. Around 11 p.m., go to bed. 2. Use a timer and set it to 3 for eight hours. Set the timer across the room Buying stuff you don't need: 1. Going out shopping for less than 2. If you have the urge to buy something, do you think that product would help me achieve my financially free goals? 3. Say what you're doing to friends, so they can help stop you.

What I want to do:

Start a profitable Real Estate Investing Business: (you can write a detailed step-by-step plan of all you need to achieve your goal). And last your own page about what you want to do with words like I want and just positive words.

You don't need to be so precise right now for long-term goals, but you should list them and list a few steps or smaller goals that you need to accomplish before you can achieve them. Always think big with the long-term goals. One good long-term target practice is to collate your goals. Place pictures of the house you want on it, places you want to go, a picture of your parents, a number of the salary you want, or something you can think of.

Learning

Knowledge builds trust and removes fear. You need to learn the ins and outs of that business if you start any kind of business. The best way I've heard about investing in real estate is to read everything about it. But you have to apply what you've learned when you know it. It's just one step to take to learn and read. There are thousands of real estate investment books on the market, and everybody has something from which you can know. Nevertheless, you don't just want to read books investing in real estate. You also want books on motivation and leadership to fill yourself. Every successful person I know if a reader and all of them spend at least thirty minutes a day reading something that will teach them how to develop their company or help themselves become better people.

Attending a Real Estate Investing Seminar.

Every weekend there are several seminars going on throughout the country. It's going to be very easy to find one if you live in a big city. If you're living in a city like Billings Montana, you may need to drive some way to find one. Another reason I suggest to go to a seminar is that they will pump you up and inspire you. You will have tons of energy and information when you get back from one of these workshops. All I want to do is go out and do a deal or ten every time I get home from one.

Such workshops will also provide you with some opportunities at a fraction of the cost to buy great real estate investment resources, technology or learning content. You will find other investors with whom you can work on a contract, even sell a deal, people who will make deals for you, and so on. Hundreds of business cards should be created, and you should try to give them all out. You never know how much you can make a business card.

Learn about the real estate market in your region. The majority of real estate investors are beginning their careers from investing where they work. When you have more experience, you can venture out. The reason for this is that we feel more comfortable with the areas and better know the areas. It's easier to get the details we need from local real estate. It's also cheaper to start investing in your local market, there are fewer travel costs, you can see what you're buying, and it can give you a sense of comfort.

You must first determine what part of the city is the best place to invest in. This can be determined by what type of property you choose to invest in. I haven't gone over the forms of real estate investments, but some of them include renovation (fixing and selling), wholesaling (finding sales and selling them to other investors), buying for sale, and some others. These are the techniques I use for most of the real estate. You need to see where other investors are buying their homes while looking at the market. Most of the best deals will be found in neighbourhood hoods of the low to the middle class. By poor I'm not referring to drug-infested war zones, I mean blue-collar safe neighbourhood hoods that may have slightly older houses and houses that are not on the higher end price side. You can now find deals in the higher priced neighbourhood hoods, but most of them are in the areas of low to middle income. If they talk to investors, they ask them some questions, such as what neighbourhoods they want, what kind of houses they purchase (3 bed 2 baths), and what they do (rehab, rent, wholesale). You shouldn't feel like a competition at other investors, but try to work with them.

There are various types of markets, such as market inflation, flat markets, and market depreciation. Markets that appreciate are markets that don't have enough houses or a very high demand for houses that cause house prices to rise. The reason for high housing demand can be due to job growth, a very desirable location, or multiple factors. Flat markets are markets with little or no growth. This means there isn't a lot of demand; just buy enough to satisfy every need. There are depreciating markets where there are many more houses to fill that house than people. This leads to a drop in house prices. This may be due to a large employer leaving the area, a natural disaster or just outside construction. Purchase in a bust and sell in a boom is an old saying. You just need to know where to find them, the deal will still be out there.

In order to become competitive, understanding the market is another element. The best source of information for you can be real estate brokers and experts in your field. Know how to use them to find out what you're in. Each market can vary from neighbourhood to neighbourhood, so make sure you're well aware of the market. I saw the same houses selling at completely different rates just a mile away.

Find a Mentor.

Having a mentor can be your greatest learning experience to help you. Mentors will help you with any concerns you may have, guide you through the investment process step by step, provide you with moral support, learn from their proven system, and network with others in the company as well. Any successful real estate developer I know says they owe a great deal of their success to the mentors they have and have in their lives. I've had one of my father's greatest mentors. Every day, he teaches me something different and encourages me to succeed.

The secret to successful investment in real estate has been uncovered!

Why did you invest in real estate? Have you read a book about it? Was that a seminar? A conference of some kind with speakers distributing information on investment in real estate, but selling courses? Have you really, really been jazzed and pumped by these basic ("not easy") concepts that a charismatic speaker has presented to you from the stage in a parallel form?

The money is in marketing the business, not in doing the business. It may take a while before you really absorb this. You may have to think about it for a while before it really sinks in. Read it again. Take a minute.

Pick up just about any book or course with real estate investing information or that is about creative real estate and you'll find the choice #1 approach to finding motivated sellers if any. What you won't find anywhere in those books, courses, or real estate investing information is the choice #2 approach, which is direct response marketing. Once in front of the target, direct response delivers the following: -A benefit-telegraphic headline -A true marketing message -An offer, or offers -A reason to respond immediately -Precise response instructions and mechanisms.

If you want to improve your real estate experience by engaging in less and more from stress, frustration, and disappointment, you should make the change.

THE WORLD OF REAL ESTATE INVESTING

U sually, in the realty company, the first thing that you need to do is to purchase a building that will not surpass your budget. This building will certainly after that be leased to a renter, and you will certainly be the renter's property owner. You as a proprietor will certainly be the one responsible for paying the costs of maintenance, tax obligations, and also as well as the home loan. You will certainly charge your renter enough, for you to be able to pay all the costs stated above. Yet do not charge your renter way too much, as the propensity is, the occupant will locate an additional residential or commercial property where he can lease at a very affordable price.

After you have made to the home mortgage as well as taxes, the renter's payment will after that become your earnings. All you have to do is find out exactly how to be an individual, for you to obtain all the revenue that you require. The good news is, the building that you got will increase its worth, which will certainly make your possession more valuable.

The negative side that you may deal with when you begin a realty organization misbehaves tenants. There are some tenants that damage buildings, particularly when you do not quadrate them. They wind up spoiling your residential or commercial properties, by damaging the doors, windows as well as such. Sometimes, when you lie in a location that is a little bit remote, having renters is virtually impossible. Yet if you recognize just how to market your property, then that would not be a problem.

If you are an individual who doesn't actually understand how to manage this type of business, you can take seminars on how you can prosper in the real estate field. You can likewise ask some of the individuals you know, that have actually enjoyed this sort of field. You can inquire regarding the issues that they had faced prior to and also what they did to conquer those problems. They can offer you some insights on what you ought to anticipate when you are just beginning with your picked area. They might also guide you to get an adviser, as this will certainly assist you in selecting certain things.

Checking out into the globe of realty is enjoyable. You just need to learn more about the ups and downs of business, for you to be well prepared. Before venturing right into this area, constantly assume first if you truly want this or otherwise. There are some people who are just being bewildered with the success tale of other realty company venture, without recognizing the problems that they could experience along the road. If you truly desire this sort of company, you require to have a great deal of courage to begin your own. Simply always keep in mind, every business has its own ups as well as downs that you have to manage.

The World of Realty Spending - The Quirks as well as the Dangers

Realty investing is all about dedicating some individual funds on a specific building with the objective of producing income by having resources appreciation, leases or leasings.

31

The term property generally refers to buildings thought about immovable like land with all the components erected or attached to it like structures or apartments. When an individual begins to get in the globe of property, he will certainly be required to handle some collection of elements like the moving as well as regulating legal rights and belongings. Understanding the turns and peculiarities of this facet of the business is essential due to the fact that it involves some lasting and substantial investments in the part of the financier. Furthermore, it benefits novices in this field to presume that the realty market is extremely vibrant and also unforeseeable.

Awaiting this quirk is needed when a private currently determines to go aboard buying structures or estate investing. Additionally, there are various approaches in which a capitalist can take part in the estate market.

The first sort of realty investing is through leasings. Individuals can decide to take part in this business with the goal of having a tenant rent the residential or commercial property they have. Via this approach, the proprietor earns money constantly from the occupants via they are still subject in handling the settlement of taxes and home mortgage. Funding appreciation or the boosting of the value of the lease of the building with time is also an advantage that the property owner can acquire. A risk of this sort of real estate is when the owner of the property can not locate any kind of feasible occupants. This will certainly bring about negative month-to-month cash flows because of all the maintenance and also mortgage settlements. As contrasted to possessing some bonds and also stocks, this area of spending requirements time, initiative, as well as perseverance from the part of the property owner.

Various other kinds of property investments are trading, investment teams, and also investment trusts. In trading, the proprietors are just called for to manage their buildings for just a short period of time like less than four months as well as concentrates to offer them within that time array. Another term for this can additionally be 'turning residential properties' which is all about needing to acquire substantial prominent and also undervalued residential properties. It is up to the property owners if they want to spend some money on maintenance and enhancement of their properties before putting it for sale once again. Investment teams, on the other hand, are a lot more like tiny mutual funds as well as are all about establishing rental properties. This involves a property manager owning some systems and a professional business handling, getting, as well as constructing out the units with some portion of the regular monthly lease going to them. An investment company, last but not least, is a firm that focuses on realty investing. They have some professions on significant exchanges as well as utilize the cash of their financiers to operate and acquire their belongings. Some benefits of this sort of investing are continuous revenue, exposure of the investors to non-residential investments.

THE REALTY CRAZE IS OVER!

If you have actually been desiring for "Turning" real estate since you have actually come across people making a fortune flipping homes - YOU ARE Far Too Late! The real estate fad has re-occurred!

Like all trends, the "Flipping Reality Trend" lasted just a short time period. This is not the first to get the rich quick trend to happen, and also it certainly won't be the last. Whether it's turning real estate, day trading stocks, reproducing ostrich eggs, or trading tulips, our history is teeming with examples of getting rich quick crazes that took the globe by a tornado and ended terribly for almost everyone.

Among the first recorded instances of a get rich fast fad was the Tulip Trend that occurred in the Netherlands in the 1600s. Tulips had actually just lately been imported from Turkey into the

Netherlands. Much of the wealthiest Dutch people started accumulating the blossoms as well as happily showed them in their homes. As time went by, the middle class took notice that this flower was so valued by the abundant, as well as likewise began accumulating the blossoms. Soon, everybody wanted tulips and also tulip light bulbs, as well as the costs, started going up. As the rates climbed, people began trading tulip bulbs as if they were a product or a stock. A person would become aware of a neighbour that had traded a tulip light bulb and made a big profit. The neighbour likewise wished to cash in on this new venture. Before long, it appeared like everybody was trading tulip light bulbs. It obtained so ludicrously, that entire estates and life-savings were traded for a single tulip light bulb!

Eventually, prices ended up being so unbelievably high that a couple of clever financiers understood that the tulip craze couldn't proceed forever. These "smart money" financiers marketed their whole supply of tulip bulbs and locked in their substantial revenues. Others followed suit, and also quickly it became apparent that the market for the light bulbs had actually gone away. Unexpectedly, every person wanted to offer their tulip bulbs, and there were no purchasers. In no time, panic offering triggered rates to drop until now; therefore, many individuals shed cash that the country's economy was thrust into a depression. So ended one of the world's initial videotaped Get Rich Quick Fads.

Get Rich Quick Crazes have continued to take place from the moment of the great tulip craze to today. The modern technology bubble of the late 1990s was an archetype of among these trends. The cost of net and innovation stocks rose. Most of these filled with air supplies were of business that had no chance to generate income. Many ideas that the rate of technology supplies would certainly remain to go up for life, because "this moment, things are different". LUDICROUS! The value of a company that can not earn money is NO! Individuals were blinded by greed as well as simply really did not realize this truth until the collision took place.

The economic situation of the USA took a dual hit in the first two years of the new millennium. First, the tech bubble ruptured taking the entire stock market down with it. After that, a small team of terrorists brought our country's economy to its knees with the assault on the twin towers of the globe trade centre. In feedback, the Fed lowered rate of interest to a 40 year reduced. This reducing of rates of interest together with the intro of kicked back loaning techniques kept our nation's economic situation solid and also opened up the possibility of owning a home (and realty investment) to a lot more Americans than in the past.

The boosted need for real estate also increased the demand for all real estate solutions. Homebuilders, real estate professionals, rehabbers, appraisers, lending institutions, and every person else in any kind of real estate relevant business succeeded. The need for residences exceeded the supply, as well as numerous clever investors, started to guess on houses. This was the birth of the house turning trend! As the smart money started to make money "turning", the middle class took notice as well as also started flipping. Soon, it seemed like everyone was turning residential or commercial property for great earnings. Demand for residences raised and it seemed like there was no limit to house rates. New investors entering the turning company increased the demand for houses, which raised the prices. The more prices went up, the much more brand-new investors entered the marketplace and also bid up prices even greater. It ended up being a vicious cycle. It got so absurd that new "investors" would certainly camp out in warm markets just for the chance to bid on pre-construction projects.

This vicious cycle continued with late 2005, at which time the real estate bubble began to decrease. The smart money recognized that rates had actually obtained unbelievably high, which the end was near. These "smart money' capitalists started selling their real estate profiles

The reality trend mores than. Demand has actually dried up, and also the number of residences on the marketplace is rising. In many areas, rates have currently started down, and this fad will certainly enhance as time goes by. The house customers and "financiers" who used interest-only financings, unfavourable amortization financings, as well as adjustable rate financings over the past couple of years will quickly have payments that are drastically greater when their advertising prices expire. Millions of these people will not have the ability to afford the greater payments and also will shed their residences to foreclosure. Every one of these millions of extra residences on the marketplace will certainly further dispirit rates and prices will likely stay low for years to find. The turning craze is finishing as unexpectedly as it started. With the lack of retail purchasers, there simply isn't a demand for flipped residences. Numerous the new "capitalists" that started flipping during the current fad will go out of business, shedding a great deal of cash.

Why have I most likely to the difficulty to write such a dismal report? Is this tale over? NO! The TRUTH is that there constantly has been as well as always will allow cash to be made in property. Nonetheless, the money to be made isn't in turning or in the latest fad!

For me, as well as others like me, the property breast will be very lucrative. You see, I am not a "Fin" as well as I was not caught up in the current real estate fad. I remain in the rental building BUSINESS as well as I supply an item that individuals ALWAYS NEED ... a place to live!

There are NUMEROUS millionaires in the United States... 7 million millionaires to be exact. A lot of those millionaires made their money possessing rental homes. Rental homes are required in all markets because people need a place to live. Actually, as the realty market becomes worse, more people will end up being occupants.

Simply today, I received a call from a lady who was looking for a residence to rent out. The reason that they required an area to rent is that their residence had been foreclosed upon. She explained that their home loan payment began at $600 each month with one of those gimmick initial rate financings. Recently, their finance repayment had actually risen to nearly $1,100 per month, and also they merely might not manage it. They supported on settlements as well as the financial institution is seizing on them. Currently, they will certainly become my occupants.

Why are services such an excellent way to make money, grow rich, develop a wide range, and retire early? The solution depends on the five various manner ins which we can earn money with leasings, usually without utilizing any one of our very own money. The five ways to earn money with rentals are:

1. Equity at closing!

Rental Characteristic REQUIREMENT is acquired at a price cut. It is almost difficult to get residential rental property at market price and after that rent it for a profit. The difference between what we pay for the property and the marketplace worth of the property is our equity, and also can total up to 10s of hundreds of dollars for each rental building!

2. Capital

With leasings, we receive a lease from our lessees each month and after that pay our operating budget as well as the home mortgage. The amount remaining is our cash flow. This is cash you can spend on living expenditures, to buy a car, for your mortgage payment or anything else that you such as. Capital is the lifeblood of every company.

3. Pay Down of Principal

Among the exciting aspects of leasings is that the tenant pays the home mortgage settlement and all costs for us. Over the regard to the financing, the mortgage will certainly be paid off as well as we'll possess your home totally free and also clear!

4. Gratitude

Historically, homes value at 3% to 5% each year. Think about this as the icing on the cake.

Let's think about a $50,000 rental property. Even if it only values 3% annually, that is one more $1,500 in equity that we grab each year! You'll keep in mind that we didn't need to do anything to get this equity. All we had to do was remain to have the residential property!

5. Tax obligation Depreciation

As if the previous four methods of generating income weren't sufficient, the government has actually pleased to allow us to drop our rental property. This can be significant cost savings on our taxes and also coincides with making added cash on your home. As of the writing of this book, properties are depreciated over a 27 1/2 year duration. This annual devaluation can be thousands of dollars each year on a solitary rental building.

Is the Globe of Real Estate Spending Right for You?

That among us does not covertly wish that one day we'll be living the American desire, not just for ourselves yet our kids and liked ones as well. While it holds true that such a wonderful lifestyle can seem out of reach sometimes thanks to life's many battles and also challenges, it's important to recognize that this is far from the instance. The American dream lives as well as it's obtainable when you tackle accomplishing it in properly.

One of the most effective methods to make your desires become a reality nowadays is property investment. Not only is investing a possibly rewarding organization, but it's one that will certainly still allow you the moment, as well as the flexibility to, in fact, appreciate your success. Allow's take a closer check out just how you can definitively tell whether or not real estate investing is a good possibility for your very own future.

Risk-Taking

Realty investment is an organization that will need you to be good on your feet when it concerns both assessing and taking dangers. This isn't an organization for individuals who such as to play things secure or stay with their regimens. This is an organization for people that think well on the fly and also that have a sixth sense when it comes to judging perspective, especially when it concerns the worth of a building they may be thinking about rehabilitating if you're a person who really flourishes on taking risks, so much the much better.

Self-Motivation

Although almost every person fantasizes about not having to endure their employer staring over their shoulders any more, only a self-starter is going to in fact be good at working in this way. As a real estate investor, you'll stay in business on your own as an independent specialist, so the only individual who will be holding you liable is you. If you're most likely to make on your own success, you have to be efficient motivating on your own to finish the job.

Marketing as well as Follow Up Skill

The investor invests a great deal of time and energy advertising themselves because their resources depend upon their capability to generate and handle top quality leads. You'll need to understand the ins and outs of using both traditional as well as contemporary approaches of self-marketing. This includes being smart in regards to social media sites advertising, one of the most important variables when it comes to developing any type of organization in the 21st century.

Individuals Ability

Last yet certainly not least, a great real estate investor is additionally great with individuals. Even if they're looking to sell, a person's properties are most likely to be unbelievably crucial to them. They're not most likely to want to market them to simply any person, so it is essential to be able to rapidly as well as definitively establish a rapport with a seller. It aids to have an all-natural knack for persuasion along with a healthy dose of personal appeal. If every one of these top qualities sounds like you, then you may wish to think actually serious about trying your hand at property financial investment. You make certain to be pleased that you did!

THE DIFFERENT TYPES OF REAL ESTATE AND HOW TO CHOOSE WHICH IS BEST FOR YOU

There are several different types of realty investments, and also it is necessary to understand what each type of financial investment is as well as what the benefits and also risks involved are. The kinds of financial investments that entail realty consist of Realty Investment Trusts.

Property Investment company is a business that sells, acquires, manages, as well as establishes land and residential or commercial properties. These REITs are established as protection that sells on all of the major exchanges much like a supply, and also straight purchases real estate by home loans or home. These trusts obtain special consideration worrying taxes as well as they normally supply a high yield and are really fluid compared to various other realty investment types. Specific people can buy this sort of real estate investment by buying shares straight on among the open exchange markets or through a financial investment broker.

The next kind of real estate investment we will check out is a realty collaboration. This is when numerous people partner together as well as pool their funds and also sources for the sole function of realty financial investment.

The trip rental building is one kind of real estate financial investment that supplies rental revenue most of the time. This kind is thought about a long-term investment, but a big benefit is that you can market this property and also obtain the value of the property regardless of the number of years you collect lease for the building. The disadvantage is that as the owner of the residential property, you are responsible for any damages, repair services, and maintenance even if the occupant created the issue. If the trouble was caused by the occupant, then you do have some remedies available in civil court for the cost of repairs and also parts. This financial investment residential property is typically rented for short time periods, and there may be periods of job where there is no rental revenue from it.

A rental home can be among the most effective real estate financial investment kinds when it involves long term earnings. This type of investment building generally gives monthly earnings unless the residential or commercial property is vacant. Regardless of the length of time, you have the financial investment home, you need to get back at least the value of your original investment, and also, for the most part, a lot more. You gather lease for as long as you possess the residential property without your investment ever before declining, so the monthly income minus expenses is a lot like a really high rate of interest repayment. Raw land realty financial investment is when a person or company purchases raw land and then earns a profit off of the natural resources of the land or creates the property.

Despite which realty financial investment kind you select, you ought to be aware of all the benefits and negative aspects of the kind you are planning to buy. Do the study as well as make your financial investment strategy, consisting of which types of realty you intend to purchase. Do your research prior to spending, and you will never be sorry afterwards.

What Kind Of Real Estate AGENT, Do You Require?

Given that, for most of us, the value of our house, represents our single - largest, financial asset, does not it make good sense, to continue intelligently, and in your best interest, when you make a decision, it's the right time, to market it? Data, constantly suggest, in a large number of instances, house owners benefit, when they capitalize, of hiring the finest quality, well - qualified, understanding, caring, REPRESENTATIVE! Whether, the primary worry, is obtaining the highest possible rate, in the fastest period of time, or attending to particular needs, objectives, and also/ or, concerns, owners benefit, when they take advantage of high quality, real estate representation.

1. Focus; actions; mindset; appropriate; capacity; analysis: A well - certified, property agent, pay keen interest, to every information, in order to guarantee, his customer's experience, is much better, etc.! He continues, with a container - do, favourable mindset, incorporated with a well - established, ability, as well as ability - established! Exactly how can any individual know, whether his understandings are apt,

as well as accurate, unless, an expert, provides a sensible evaluation?

2. Greater results: Greater results arise from better emphasis, and also highlighting a certain building's stamina, while attending to locations of weakness, so potential, professional purchasers, are more determined, to buy the specific home!

3. Initiatives; effects; effective; excellence; endurance: Efficiently, advertising and marketing and also offering a residence, requires positioning one's initiatives, where it will certainly develop the most effective results! An efficient agent, strives to supply solution, based on authentic excellence, and also identifies, the property transaction period, always has specific challenges, as well as, calls for the endurance, and also capacity, to continue, in a positive, focused way!

4. Demands; a particular niche: During a house owner's interview procedure, to determine, which agent, to work with, the representative has to learn, discover, and comprehend a client's demands, while identifying the particular niche, in regards

to prospective customers, and comparative buildings!

5. Time - evaluated; prompt: A seasoned representative, based on his knowledge, experience, and also competence, develops the judgment, as well as, hopefully, wisdom, to proceed, with time-examined concepts, and also approaches. To obtain one of the most preferable outcomes, it's important, for agents, to constantly, continue, in a well - taken into consideration, timely way, so prospective purchasers, and also their agents, really feel welcome, and also a lot more proper, to pick, your specific home!

With all the representatives, in most locations, does not it make sense, to work with someone, that will make a meaningful difference, right, in regards to the possible results? Will you put in the time, to recognize, the appropriate individual, for your needs?

Property Sales Agents - Exactly How to Choose One That Would Certainly Function Well for You

There are a lot of realty agents that agree to benefit you available. However, locating the one that would work out things well for you is another story. The selection is frequently the hardest. While there perhaps lots of brokers and agents that are greater than willing to provide their services, you can never be sure of their efficiency unless you have placed them on trial.

Therefore, it is best to discover a property sales agent that can really rotate things in his own hands as well as give you the very best of what your home and also the other problems could provide.

The efficiency of a property sales representative is specified by different variables. For instance, their official education and learning and the years of training they have actually undergone can have substantial results on your assurance for the best offers. Nonetheless, those two aspects do not tell every little thing. Certain conditions can additionally promote their ideal efficiency, and various other aspects of realty sales might add largely to the end result of your sale.

Prior to you get on with your search for the realty sales representatives of the upper quality, you must recognize first the terms that are usually used mutually in business.

Real estate sales agents and also brokers are various from each various other. The brokers are more like companies that offer the solutions of a variety of agents who are directly attached to their business as freelancers or employees. The agents, however, are the primary labour force of such property brokers. As implied in our meaning above, they might be functioning solo, or they are being handled by certain businesses or firms that have a larger extent of services. A real estate professional, on the other hand, is not so distinctive with realty sales agents. Nevertheless, they still vary considering that the real estate agents are those that have extra certification originating from the nationwide Association of Realtors.

Having stated that, we can after that think that you have even more defined standards on that or what to pick when trying to find the solutions of a person or an institution to offer or advertise the sales of your residential property.

Yet the titles are not so affective of the character your property sales agent must-have. It is true that it's not typically easy to locate extremely devoted and also committed people to help your residential property. They are available in scarce number however are nonetheless worth searching for. Here are some ideas for you to help you in seeking the services of being reliable as well as effective real estate sales agent:

Remember that there are various types of organizations that supply you the services genuine estate sales. Yet the titles ought to not be your main point for judging which firm or individual you should be consulting with. What issues most is that you select the most effective carrying out people to secure the easy selling of your residential property.

Take into consideration also the sort of representation you are after. Usually, property sales are the seller's agents. They only represent the wagers' passion of their clients as well as go no better than that unless they want to reroute such passion in the direction of much more efficient and also much better transactions.

It will deserve it if you are most likely to do some research. While a lot of realty sales representatives as well as brokers have internet sites that you can easily access, there is absolutely nothing far much better than personally speaking to these people to offer you your benefits and also downsides when your contract begins.

Dave Grandone

NICHES AND STRATEGIES FOR REAL ESTATE INVESTMENT

R ealty is simply a tool you use in planning a general approach to living a well balanced and also enjoyable life. As soon as you discover your sweet area, in reality, you'll be one action more detailed to being successful with close to perfect performance in a delightful and flourishing venture.

Presently you'll locate that the world is on sale as well as everything is negotiable, your capacity to locate, discuss, framework, handle and market real property is crucial to cashing substantial checks in the process. afterwards

If you're presently utilized then maintain that position until your real estate earnings surpass your month-to-month take away pay by two times your existing wage, then bank six months' worth of incomes before you consider leaving that old 9 to 5 in favour of fulltime investing. You might also pick to make use of property investing as an additional earnings stream while you maintain the normal J.O.B. (Simply Over Broke). It is recommended that you have seven independent streams of earnings in order to be protected versus unforeseen circumstances that cause phase 11 truly.

Policy primary is "Keep your overhead reduced" Your brand-new offices will certainly be considered your cars and truck, your residence and also neighbourhood public areas, these are all great places to perform general tasks as well as are considered generally appropriate workrooms for the mobile investor in today's real estate video game.

Remember this expression 'There are Treasures in Particular niche's" as well as there are an excellent numerous specialized to pick from in property, you need to make every effort to become a specialist in 2 or 3 areas of competence yet not numerous that you fail to grasp the fundamentals of each particular niche. You don't want to be a one technique pony yet you don't want to be the typical jack of all trades and also a master of none either.

You heard that all effective people are frequently masters of time administration; it will certainly serve you well to gain from the best right from the beginning while you avoid continuously looking for brand-new mentors to instruct within the same subject areas. Try to Restrict the number of different guides that you receive from contending resources so that you can preserve your concentrate on one tried and tested detailed technique that has currently been verified to function by adhering to an existing plan, there is no demand to recreate the wheel, use existing systems to utilize and compound your success and also progression.

Begin by finding an overview, somebody that has already looked into, found and validated certified resources that are verified success designs, from here, you can begin developing your group. Every Person Achieves Much More. There is no such point as competitors; you should consider it a co-operating competition. There is lots of chance for everyone, don't allow a scarcity attitude to spoil your journey.

There is an old saying in the property as well as it states" You get paid when you fix an issue" seek to be a problem solver and also a service supplier throughout your networks and also areas of procedure, and you'll discover greater possibilities to be of service throughout your day.

Right here are a few of the choices you need to provide a solution in real estate: bird-dogging, foreclosure investing, creative financing, seller funding, owner funding, no cash down, private financing, notes & mortgages, commercial, property, raw land, judgments, liens, turning, wholesaling, sub2, auctions, probate, lease purchase, alternatives, tax obligation techniques as well as a lot much more.

The trick is personal goal setting as well as we'll make it very easy, starting with simply 30 minutes a day to review one chapter of real estate educational materials to assist you completely prepare within 90 days to start doing successful deals while conserving you time, cash and frustration.

Think it or not, it just takes a short while to understand the principles, seal the principles, impart the fundamentals as well as begin to develop your network while designing your plans as well as preparing to execute your method utilizing accurate methods to possess your particular niche in the property.

Dave Grandone

Wholesaling - A Strategy For Real Estate Investors

The technique of wholesaling houses is among the most well-defined and also uncomplicated investing techniques out there. It is just situating a deal residential property and passing it on to deal hunters. The period it takes from situating a motivated vendor to closing is likewise one of the shortest durations out of all the other particular niches in property investing. Realty investing is an exceptional way to make a living, yet before you begin wholesaling houses for a living, you must take a little time to be educated what it's everything about.

Wholesaling has actually been around for a while, but over the last few years it has actually become a lot more well-known and also appropriate - and as opposed to what some people believe, it is totally legal. And with the ideal information, insight and also get in touches with it can be a lucrative obstacle.

Don't be greedy:

Possibly one of the most useful issues that you need to bear in mind as you choose to wholesale is your deal hunter must get the bulk of the bargain! This is vital given that your buyer will be the one to spend for as well as repair the building.

There has to be enough chance in the purchase for your customer to do this as well as still hold on to a great amount of cash for squander and/or equity.

This does not imply that you locate homes and give them away for $1,000. If you did that, you would be an attendant, not a wholesaler. Your revenue will certainly vary relying on the home, but the much better you are at locating deals and also putting together deals, the greater your earnings will be - while still preserving a tremendous profit for your buyer.

Why do customers not discover their very own deals?

On the outside, it might appear as if realty wholesaling is a little unneeded. It feels like the buyer could without any problem situate inexpensive offers on his or her very own without any demand for an intermediary. These bargain hunters do look for bargains on their own, yet they are not able to reveal all of the terrific bargains. The sort of buyers that seek out wholesale bargains is typically always on the lookout for more deals, rehabbing them as well as offering them on the typical home market.

And also, who wouldn't jump at a home that's still offered to them at method under the market worth?

In Review, realty wholesaling can be a very uncomplicated venture for that specific merely starting in real estate. You establish a process for bringing in wholesale leads, develop a buyers listing and also begin appointing agreements to your customers. It truly is very easy once you get the process began.

Real Estate Investments-Discover the Power of Using a First-Rate Newspaper Ad

Although there are plenty of advertising tools you can use to find motivated buyers, there's plenty of power to use a first-rate newspaper ad to improve your quest and investment business.

Here are a few things to consider when making a newspaper ad for the first time as well as the form of advertising to use.

Target Your Market • Consider Your Niche: First, you're going to decide what kind of market you're trying to target. Decide on your niche and decide if it is targeted at low, medium or high-end properties. The reason I say this is that different client groups are responding to different ad styles.

• Decide your plan: decide how much you want to spend on the advertising budget of your newspaper. This is an important consideration as it will cost considerably more than a simple classified ad for a whole published post. You don't want to delete your plan if you're confused and then you don't have any answers.

Know Your Audience. Understand who your target is and figure out how much they are trying to solve and why they may be inspired to sell as much as possible. Include information in the commercial that explains the solution to your problem instantly and top it off with a headline that catches attention. With this phase, most beginning real estate investors forget to do their homework and then muddle up the ad despite needless graphics and far too many details. Make sure the ad is straightforward and simple, and remember testing, testing, and testing again.

Keep up with the market conditions in the neighbourhood where you want to invest in trying to determine the best time when people might be willing to sell. Generally, more people read the newspaper's weekend edition which costs more to advertise, but during the week you may also find inspired sellers through ads, depending on the market you're trying to target.

One Time Will Not Produce Results Just as it is a rule of thumb in your real estate marketing plan to maintain continuity, you must pass this belief to your ads for newspapers. Keep in mind that one time ads will not do the trick. To put more than one ad and then repeat this process regularly, you will need to position your advertising budget. Make sure you have a tactical plan to place the ads so you can monitor the effects and then change as needed. It includes experimenting within each ad you generate with various headlines and varying content. Keep track of what works and what doesn't work as well as all the marketing strategies. With your future marketing efforts, it will save you a lot of time and money and provide you with a continuous flow of inspired sellers.

How to Use a Customers Checklist For Real Estate Spending

Using customers listing in property investing can be challenging or really basic if you approach it appropriately. The complicated component comes when you don't recognize the focus as well as principal of the list. The straightforward part is how you accumulate the names for the listing.

A purchasers checklist is utilized to offer residential properties to buyers, so the vendor does not need to wait for people ahead to the property through extensive marketing. Costly advertising and marketing consist of real estate agent ® compensations. Even at a 5% payment on a sale, this totals up to $25,000 each year on just five sales at $100,000 each. Multiply this by 20, 50 or 100 residential or commercial properties, and also the numbers are staggering.

Additionally, real estate professionals typically utilize the Multiple Listing Solution ("MLS") to advertise for other real estate professionals ® to market the residential property. These other representatives bring their very own purchasers to see the home as well as are paid 1/2 of the compensation. All this takes time which can extend right into months or years depending on the area and also the rate of the home. Investors have to sell as promptly as feasible to reduce they bring costs and also get their profit out.

Real estate investors have actually become proficient in developing ways to offer homes very swiftly without paying real estate professionals compensation. The most remarkable of these is making use of a buyers list of "hungry" buyers that have formerly revealed a rate of interest in getting wholesale houses, rental units and even rehabbed residential properties that are ready to move in for retail customers.

The purchaser's list is essential to the ongoing success of every real estate investor. Sadly, the majority of do not understand this up until they have to sell their buildings to a tiny group of purchasers that are not in a competitive bidding situation. This causes the capitalist not obtaining as large a profit as he could if the sale was in an affordable advertising scenario.

As the financier constructs his purchaser's list, he must classify his point of view buyers right into "sub-groups" that are essentially niche buyers. These consist of, yet are not limited to, property owners, dealers, rehabbers, end-buyers. Each of these groups of purchasers will certainly pay various costs for the very same residential or commercial property if it fits their details needs. For example, wholesalers will pay the least due to their intending to re-sell the property yet again, so they have to have adequate spread to make a profit.

Rehabbers will certainly pay more than wholesalers because they are the target audience for dealers as well as they are considering the after fixed value ("ARV") for their bigger spreads. Landlords are concentrated on their return on investment ("ROI") from rental income and will usually pay more than wholesalers or rehabbers. Finally, the end-buyers are where the biggest revenue exists. End-buyers are house owners who are buying the residential or commercial property to stay in themselves.

Each of the numerous types of point of view purchasers can be promoted for or found using normal financier strategies. There are over 25 of these techniques that will certainly find hungry customers that are simply waiting to get the investor's home. The end-buyers are fickle in the feeling that when they want a residence to reside in, they remain to search up until they discover one. The proprietors are somewhat fussy because they do not constantly have financing in place to purchase even more devices. Dealers and also rehabbers are usually constantly "ready to purchase" if the residential property is a good deal.

The investor who constructs his listing has to be equally familiar with discovering homes to offer his point of view purchasers - even when he does not have any of his very own. He can deal with other wholesalers, rehabbers as well as property managers to market their properties and companion in the profits if a customer originates from his checklist. By offering buildings that are "good deals" as regularly as feasible, he can earn a living without needing to discover, rehab and re-sell to the retail market.

Great Strategies to Develop Plentiful Wealth With Real Estate

Real riches are not having an abundance of cash; it is controlling a system that produces a continuous circulation of plentiful money! As I often claim in my seminars as well as forums, "The secret to the wide range is not money -it is cashflow!" To put it simply, the key to riches is managing a system that generates a constant and also a constant supply of money. The trick to obtaining riches actually lies in obtaining possessions that create wealth.

There are three necessary, non-negotiable parts in order for a wealth development system to work. These three important parts are

1. A detailed plan to obtain resources (simply put -cash).

2. The growth of unrelenting as well as strenuous monetary behaviours.

3. An easy-to-follow plan on how to get income-producing properties (in other words -cashflow).

Let me describe exactly how investing in real estate can function as your individual wealth creation system.

One technique is: "Quick-Cash Investing" This is where a normal residence is acquired at a wholesale cost and after that re-sealed as a list price. You can make good money with this approach and have the ability to get yourself began on the course to wealth development. Quick Cash money offers you the influx of money you may require to clear old debt and obtain your hands on capital for Cash Flow investing.

Another approach is: "Cashflow Spending After developing healthy and balanced money routines and also safeguarding resources, you must start Cashflow investing. This is where you utilize your capital to buy cashflow creating property assets to develop a healthy form of easy income. Don't wait. Obtain enlightened concerning the techniques as well as approaches that you can make use of to become an active and also effective real estate investor, and start building your personal riches production system today. The Power of Beliefs You require to have a company hold of the concerns that will certainly affect your success in today's world. Because that is the case, I have chosen to expose a big misconception concerning money that has actually been given from generation to generation. This myth regarding money has actually affected the way millions of individuals see money and has actually kept plenty of individuals from ever before achieving their individual economic liberty. I learned, many years ago, that getting wealth and also enjoying riches are truly two various points. Earning money is not really all that hard. It is merely an issue of establishing your niche and also obtaining your investments correctly. Now, you would assume that this is the end of the tale, yet it isn't. Because individuals think certain features of money, they are after that triggered by their personal psychology to practice particular actions once they get that cash. Some people attain wide range and afterwards really feel guilty for having it. They end up threatening their monetary routines to the point that they shed their wealth swiftly to make sure that they don't have to manage the inner anxiety of having it. This subconscious method of self-disruption keeps them from ever before actually attaining their full monetary capacity. The fact is that what we believe about cash dramatically affects not just our capability to get it, yet additionally our ability to maintain it. The actual distinction between abundant people as well as bad people is not just how much cash they make; it is how much of the cash they keep! I desire you to be able to acquire a wide range as well as maintain it to be utilized for your personal satisfaction. Because that holds true, I wish to expose some cash myths with you. Let's quickly have a look at a cash misconception now! There is just a lot of money to walk around. The majority of the financial practices of the largest corporations are influenced by the thought that there is just so much riches around to be acquired in today's world. The concept behind this idea is the idea that when every one of the globe's wide range is seized, then those who do not have wealth will certainly find themselves not able to acquire any more of it. This is a tired and false misconception. Many people think that money is a limited point, but cash isn't a point at all. Money is actually simply an idea -it is an abstract device used to gauge the value of something. Individuals believe the idea that a hundred-dollar note deserves greater than a fifty-dollar note, although the real value of the paper, ink as well as printing costs behind them are roughly the same! Money is not a thing, it is a suggestion and also there is a lot of it available for everyone that intends to make an effort to develop strong techniques for acquiring it. Cash is NOT a scarce or finite source. Cash is an abundant idea. It is very important to recognize that there is plenty of cash out there for everyone since it takes away the anxiousness that people that are trying to develop an economic lot of money experience when they see other individuals around attempting to generate income also.

DECIDING WHETHER TO SELL OR NOT

This might not be straightforward to agree to sell your home, but this choice will potentially turn into a nightmare. It is really difficult to find the right buyer, and it may take a great deal of time, particularly during the winter months when the demand starts to slow down. Many buyers purchase a new home with a mortgage, and it's more possible that you will have to wait for him or her to get accepted for the loan until the investor informs you that he or she decides to buy the property. You might want to consider selling the house to a real estate investor-you'll get the money straight away, and the entire thing would be less complicated because they will get their portion of the paperwork completed very fast.

The client isn't the only one to have the documentation finished. You can check at what documentation is expected of you-tax paid reports, land information, financial documents, definition of legal properties, and likely by-laws for homeowners. Keeping the papers in order will take you some time, it would be easier if you hadn't tried to do so before closing. It would be really easy to displace or destroy records so it takes the organizations a while to bring you a collection of fresh ones (this could cost you money too).

Going at the real estate developers will be a wise thing to do. Selling your property to such a buyer can be better than charging lots of money to your broker-they 're still wealthy enough, why make them wealthier even?

Asking yourself "Will I need to sell my house? "The good news is that you will quickly negotiate the labyrinth of sales with a little planning, reliable knowledge and an outstanding real estate agent that can direct you.

Sellers are strongly favoured by the existing real estate environment, so now might be a perfect moment to sell your house.

Latest figures from the National Association of Realtors indicate that current single-family home values have risen over the last year in more than 80 per cent of metropolitan areas. According to NAR's chief economist, Lawrence Yun, the rapid growth is partly attributed to "a quicker speed of home selling in the middle of languishing inventory ratios." Pair this with nearly record-low mortgage rates, rising work opportunities, and sluggish new home development, and you've got plenty of buyers without enough homes to purchase.

It's nice to realize with such a big demand for buyers that you will potentially sell your house easily and get a decent deal, but is that incentive enough to place it on demand?

There are a few precautions you can take before you put up the "For Sale" sign.

Start With Your Goals

If you're like other people, the choice to sell your home is based on a particular combination of variables. Understanding what such considerations are is the first move in deciding the housing goals.

Real estate brokers believe that the biggest predictor of becoming a happy investor is understanding that you're selling.

Richard Schulman, a leading Los Angeles real estate specialist, refers to establishing targets as the starting point for every real estate consultation.

"For sellers, the most critical aspect is to get as much focus on their objectives as possible. I just want to ask why they're selling their home.'

According to Schulman, as an advisor, having customers establish reasonable targets is his work-even though it does n't include sales.

"Let's presume the consumer needs to purchase a bigger house. That's fine, but if they can't get a loan for the bigger property, there's no point in selling the one they've received. "On any way, selling the home needs to make sense to you. A truthful and professional real estate agent will help you sort your sale grounds and come up with a solution that fits your needs. You will set realistic targets with their support-and a little diligence on your part.

Set Goals by Finding Your "Why"

Below we've developed a few assessments and drills to help you explain your housing objectives and prioritize them. That's a tripartite operation.

Determine if you need to sell your house, and/or want to.

Check the finances.

Meet an accomplished real estate agent in your city.

Find your desires, your wishes and your resources as the foundation blocks of your ambitions for sale. Start with the greatest needs, then add your desires to the order of priority, and use your financial identity as a mirror to see it all through.

Of example, desires always carry greater weight than you would want, so if you have a dream list that your new home cannot fulfil, don't dismiss them.

The "Need to Sell" Test

Identify any infrastructure needs that could be addressed by selling and get a head start on your first meeting with your agent; some of the most popular are below.

- Question 1: Are you changing jobs?

- Question 2: Is your family size changing?

- Question 3: Are you retiring?

- Question 4: Are you experiencing new health issues?

- Question 5: Is your home or neighbourhood unsafe?

- Question 6: Is your area too noisy, congested, or inconvenient?

- Question 7: Has your income significantly decreased?

Experiencing one or more of those big adjustments in your life may mean selling your home is your only choice or even a requirement. Whether the new work adds thirty minutes to your drive or whether a doctor in another region might help handle your health issues, the answer could be to sell.

At the other side, whether you have a newborn on the way or retirement is around the corner, perhaps with a few changes may be your new home will still be able to satisfy your needs. That way, if you set practical real estate goals and explore all the possibilities with your real estate agent, you'll be more effective.

Would Goldilocks remember? The flaxen-haired girl wanted to eat something, but that wasn't enough; she wanted to eat the best porridge bowl while seated in the perfect chair, accompanied by a nap in the perfect room. Goldilocks had both desires and expectations, so she made sure that she had them. You deserve nothing less, so let's move on to the "wants" that may nudge you into selling your home. Of new sales, the National Association of Realtors records a combination of needs and wants: "... for younger buyers many want to move to a larger home to support work transfer. By contrast, others want to be closer to friends and family with older homeowners to buy a smaller home because of retirement. "You could find yourself somewhere in the centre, and that's all right.

You should have an educated discussion with your real estate agent armed with the arguments you want to sell. These experts can help you understand why you are selling and set concrete goals based on their local business expertise and understanding.

The following exercises are intended to help you build targets that are focused on your unique results. A mix of reasons undoubtedly motivates you to sell. With that in mind, resist the temptation of simply responding "yes" or "no."

Rather, think of this as a starting point for discussion (especially if more than one individual makes the decision to sell). Know that your real estate agent will use your responses to decide whether selling is the best option.

The "Want to Sell" Test

Your responses here should represent your dream lifestyle, how it varies from your current circumstance and what you're searching for in a new house. Such questions are more complex, which would, therefore, take longer to respond. Don't restrict yourself; just take these as triggers to help you think more creatively of what your home could look like.

- Question 1: Is your commute too long or too expensive?

- Question 2: Are you itching for a bigger, nicer home?

- Question 3: Are you looking for a better school system?

- Question 4: Are you having trouble with your neighbours?

- Question 5: Are you sick of the weather in your area?

- Question 6: Would you like to be closer to the things that matter to you?

In comparison to the previous test's "needs," responding "yes" or "maybe" in this segment does not mean the sale is your only choice. You might be forced to wait for disputes with your neighbour or remodel your new home to provide the room or facilities you are searching for.

Very possibly, you'll notice you need further detail to decide whether your "wants" are important enough to sell your house. That is where recruiting a professional real estate agent pays off – their industry experience also often applies to home design and development, and they can lead you on alternate strategies to achieve your objectives. You will have some research to do before you make the call for advice.

Homework Lesson 1: Prioritize Your Needs and Wants

Use your survey responses as a point of reference, describe your housing requirements and desire on different lists. Prioritize your lists by positioning your desires at the end, then order your requests according to their value. Look out not to compare the two! It's tempting to encourage you to take over your list because they're always more enjoyable-the bigger kitchen will be great, but are you able to risk a shorter ride to get it? Instead, a chart of samples might look like this:

- NEED: Move closer to family

- NEED: More space for baby on the way

- WANT: Quiet neighbourhood

- WANT: Walking distance to restaurants and schools

- WANT: Large backyard

- WANT: Updated kitchen

Dale Boutiette, San Francisco 's leading real estate company, offers two latest ways of directing its buyers around the difficult terrain of needs, requires and setting targets.

"A young couple purchased and leased a condo downtown in 2008 but had trouble locating tenants at a higher price level. We were talking about sales, and I sent them a business study. The study indicated that they would sell at first glance-competitive results revealed that they could increase their initial expenditure. But as I looked further, I found sales in their building weren't as solid so they definitely wouldn't be having a decent deal.

Three questions I asked them: Can you make a profit from rent? Hey. Would you want to be a landlord? No. Do you find real estate a good investment in your area? Sure. Selling with such responses made little sense.

The best decision has been to offer for another pair in a similar case. It was a hellish drive and a baby that tilted the balance here. The same three questions I posed to them; they were no longer involved in becoming tenants, so they agreed to sell.

The stories of Boutiette are good reminders that the "why" of each seller is unique to them, and is a combination of needs, wants and finances. The reports often illustrate the benefits of having an accomplished real estate consultant in the decision-making cycle!

Homework Lesson 2: Conduct a Financial Assessment

Knowing your wishes and needs is a pretty good starting point, but you will also need to create realistic financial expectations to get a complete picture of your objectives. Here are a few tips to get you going on what may be a difficult task:

- **Your budget.** Creating or checking a report or the real expenses by gathering a few months' receipts. Should not neglect to apply to interest premiums, recurring housekeeping costs and royalties.

- **Home value estimate.** This should give you a general understanding of what to expect from a deal. To achieve an approximate number, using the HomeLight Home Value Estimator (it selects five separate numbers across a selection online). Yet keep in mind that you can only get a reliable quote from a real estate agent.

- **Real estate agent.** I realize it sounds like a cracked record, but it's irreplaceable knowledge that a strong agent brings to the table. Together you can build a net sheet (a helpful overview of your existing mortgage, an estimation of the sale price and the sales costs in your region). You will also perform a detailed comparative review of the recently sold homes in your region to help you build your selling targets.

Homework Lesson 3: Find the Best Real Estate Agent in Your Area

Even if you are only exploring the sale waters, finding a successful real estate agent in your region should be your next move. A successful agent is not going to mind you are not trying to sell your home. On the contrary, a good agent takes more care to make the right decision for you than to get a commission.

Boutiette has chalked his performance to first position clients: "The most popular form of a real estate agent is to chase transactions. Yet it's really partnership dependent on our approach. The distinction is that my goal is to respect the partnership with the customer or seller in such a manner that they recognize that their needs come before mine. We had a year when referrals were 100 per cent of our transactions – that's unheard of.

Look for a real estate agent whose biggest concern is what's best for you; who's got an established track record of closing deals in your area; and who's happy customers you can use as references.

The Decision is Yours (But You Don't Need to Make it Alone)

You will set clear targets and reasonable standards, guided by a real estate professional's knowledge and skills, for a fully positive decision on whether to sell.

Derek Oie, Chino Hills, CA 's top real estate agent, continues his client partnership with "the million-dollar question" – Why did you want to sell it? Oie says it's important to consider the purpose of a vendor and "to recognize that they want to sell." Nowadays, the most popular excuse buyers give having a better, nicer house. Oie says there to initiate the dialogue, but it's never that easy. As evidence he shares a recent couple 's story:

"They came to me needing to improve their location and house. Your fees go up every time you deal. We looked at their budgets and existing funding and concluded that waiting was the route to reach their goals. They began a savings plan and are budgeting for a higher rate of mortgages. This would have been immoral to order them to sell until they're willing.'

Take your time, after you have finished the aforementioned tests, to select a relationship-oriented and effective real estate agent to make sense of your circumstance better. Never should selling a home be a cookie-cutter experience. Work with someone willing to customize their approach to your goals to ensure a satisfying process and sale.

Financial Considerations Of Selling Your Home: Should You Sell Your House?

With the New Year's turn, many people will consider selling their house and seeking a new one. They 're wondering, "Will I sell my house, or is it time to move? Traditionally speaking, the early part of the year was a perfect time to sell your home.

Usually, consumers are back on the market during the holidays, hunting for homes. But even though it's not the beginning of the new year, spring will quickly be on us, and the demand will start up at the right place and the right price with prospective customers searching for the perfect home. So, if you are talking about selling your home, is that the correct decision? Verily, there really isn't a right solution, or one size fits all approach to suit all conditions.

This can vary in various circumstances, and you have to consider and prepare a little bit to decide what makes sense to you.

Making It About The Money
Will you profit on the sale of your existing home?

A decent real estate agent would typically ask you how much you intend to sell your old home for and what is the best price you will expect for a new property?

It is important to run a few numbers in order to find out. Consider certain expenses (hint: to get figures on a prior settlement statement):

- Real estate sales commissions

- Fees paid at closing: In looking at my last settlement statement, we paid some

- Title charges

- Government recording and transfer charges

- Any additional settlement charges

- Pay off for existing mortgage

- Home repairs if this is included in the sales contract. Or, perhaps you need to make repairs before putting your house on the market.

- Pre-sale preparations such as landscaping, painting, etc.

You'll need to learn how much your house is worth, and what you're going to sell it for. Your real estate agent will support you by taking comps to show you what other houses in your neighbourhood are going for. You may use services like zillow.com to get ideas too.

If you have great estimated costs and a reasonable sales price, you should be possible to ascertain whether you can expect to walk away with any profit from the deal or get back the cash that went into buying your house.

There is always a buyer, but the price has to be right.

Remember you can't simply list your house for whatever your heart wants. The fundamental theory of the property sector follows. There is a price point for each area that people buy in unless it's a special circumstance. You just need to find that price point and suggest whether or not it will leave you with a profit or a loss in view of the costs.

How much will it cost to get into the new house?

When you realize how many you 're going to spend with the home selling, remember the expenses of moving into a new place:

- Costs associated with the new loan

- Title charges

- Government recording and transfer charges

- Prepaid expenses such as insurance and taxes or reserves deposited with the lender

- Moving costs

- New house purchases (such as window coverings (if not a new house).

Do you still have some cash left for a down payment after those cost? If so (or not), how much house you can manage will be decided. If you follow the mortgage law of Dave Ramsey in which interest payment, taxes and benefits can not surpass 25 per cent of your monthly take-home pay, you would be able to calculate the buying amount required to make those percentages function.

7 Signs You're Ready To Sell Your House

Would I want to sell my house? If you have been asking yourself this query lately, we have good news: It's a big seller area! Restricted inventory tends to push up house values, and the new report from the Regional Association of Realtors reveals that for less than a month, almost half of the newly acquired homes remain on the market.

The decision to sell the house is of necessity not based purely on business factors. You have to take into consideration the particular situation — and this is when professional guidance comes in handy.

Below are seven indicators the house is ready to sell:

1. You've got equity on your side.

For most buyers, getting equipped financially to sell the house is down to one factor: equity. Throughout the 2008–09 mortgage crisis, millions of homeowners found themselves with negative equity, which implied they owed more than they paid on their properties.

Obviously, because you have zero equity, selling your house is a terrible idea. That's called a short sale. It's better to break even on your home sale, but it's not perfect yet. When you consider yourself in that case, don't sell because you have to stop fraud or foreclosure.

Property prices have been increasing over the past number of years — by leaps and strides in several cases — and this ensures most investors are creating equity. Their houses are now worth more than they owe them, and this trend will continue as they pay down their debts, and property prices continue to rise.

It may seem difficult to find out how much equity you have, but calculations are really easy. This is the way it works:

Next, snatch the new mortgage document and check the present balance on the mortgage.

You would, therefore, need to learn the worth of your house. While utilizing estimates from online appraisal platforms is enticing to decide how much your house is worth, they aren't necessarily reliable. To get the highest answer, ask an accomplished real estate agent to perform a free, comparative market analysis (CMA).

Simply subtract your current mortgage balance from the estimated market value of your home once you have these two numbers in hand. The gap should give you a clear perspective on how much money you ought to deal with.

How much equity is needed, then? In the very least, you want ample money to pay off the new debt and plenty left over to have a down payment of 20 per cent. But if the selling will still offset the cost of closure, travel costs and even bigger down payment — that's great. Setting 20 per cent or so down on the house often holds private mortgage insurance (PMI) at bay. That will save you hundreds of dollars annually!

2. You're out of debt with cash in the bank.

When the first trip around the home-buying block you didn't get all of the financial ducks in a row, you've already experienced a few lessons the hard way. Like Murphy was able to detect "broke" from miles out. If something might go bad, it should! Put those insights to good use and be the next go-round as a money-smart home buyer!

Start by having a close look at your finances. If you have paid down all of your non-hypothecary loans and have three or six months of expenditures in your emergency fund, it's a positive indication that you are financially stable enough to buy a house again.

3. You can afford to buy a home that fits your lifestyle better.

Another aspect to remember is how much your house meets your everyday needs. You could possibly use another (or even two) bedroom to accommodate your growing family. Or maybe all of your children have moved out, and you're ready to downsize. Empty nesters will greatly benefit from sales at low prices. Selling a large house, charging cash for a smaller one, and saving the remainder for your retirement, is easy.

If you scale up or down, make sure that your mortgage blends in with your budget.

4. You can cash-flow the move.

Don't get so swept away with your new home 's anticipation that you fail to keep in mind the risk of losing the present one. Hiring specialist movers? Save cash to cover the cost of packaging and carrying away your products.

You should save a little more to ready your current position for prime time. Focus on paint, curb appeal, plus kitchen and bath upgrades to your home improvement dollars. A little bit of fresh paint and elbow grease will create a perfect impact a long way and have the house sold fast!

Would you like a free tip which doesn't cost a dime? Flush the noise away. Neat wardrobes and clean shelves make your home look bigger!

5. You're emotionally ready to sell.

If the statistics show that you are financially ready for a change, perfect! Yet don't forget — selling your home is likewise an emotional problem. Take a minute to answer only a couple more questions before you plant the "For Sale" sign in the front yard:

- Are you able to bring your house able for household hunters into work?

- Are you dedicated to having it weeks or months ready for a show?

- Are you prepared to hear why potential buyers think your home isn't perfect?

- Are you ready to negotiate honestly — and sometimes hardball — on what buyers are willing to pay for your home?

- Are you very able to step out and abandon the location where memories were created by your family?

Don't get us wrong; we don't want to speak to you about selling a house! We only want you to be completely informed as you want to step on to your family's next level in existence.

A competent real estate agent will give a clear idea of what it is like to sell your house, as well as help you discern whether it is now time for you, financially and emotionally.

6. You Understand the Market (a Little Bit)

Nobody can guess how the housing market is going to work. But for new homes, the Regional Organization of Realtors predicts moderate development in 2018. Amid increasing mortgage costs, home purchases are expected to rise by about 7% in 2018, with median prices growing by 5%.

Home Values Are Riding High

Despite prices up and levels down on mortgages, many tenants are trying to purchase their first house. There is just one problem: They have trouble locating homes for rent within their price range.

However, according to studies, the industry currently has 20 per cent less entrance-level homes than there are last year this date. When the economy was down, a number of buyers picked up bargains on entry-level homes and converted them into a rental property.

You learned all about supply and demand as you studied economics in college. If production is down and competition is increasing, costs are still moving upward. Which means more than you thought your home would be worth. Take all the numbers:

- According to the National Realtors Association, the total number of US houses on the market is just 34 days, four fewer than last year.

- New starter homes lists are 8 per cent smaller than ads, indicating there are more house hunters eligible for rent than houses.

In other words, for just about any home seller, the market is hot — but especially if you have a starter home to sell.

7. You Have a Real Estate Agent

Until selling your home this year, it is important to understand the reasons already listed. Just note, it's a special real estate market — and so is your financial condition. To find out how the 2018 housing market is shaping up in your city, visit an expert real estate agent, and you can determine whether a transaction makes financial sense for your family.

You should trust a friend with a career to give objective guidance so you can decide what's right for you and your budget. A strong salesman places support above sales — but when it is time to move, he understands how to get it finished.

That's a huge deal to sell your house. A real estate agent performs more than just book home presentations. We carry expertise and faith to the table while coping with their various work responsibilities, including:

- Inform you on upgrades or repairs to make your house more appealing.

- Helping you fix a house rent.

- Advertise the house, so it receives as much attention as possible from prospective buyers.

- Projection of displays for prospective customers.

- Asking you when you are making deals.

- Gathering all the required paperwork.

MARKETING YOUR HOUSE FOR SALE

W hen it comes to advertising your home for sale, often owners who actually want to sell their homes face the difficulty of promoting their homes for maximum exposure. For this cause, using a qualified realtor is a good idea.

When it comes to selling a home, marketing is everything. Despite proper exposure, the interest of prospective buyers is increasingly difficult. An agent will deliver an already-established online presence and is one of the better ways for your home to receive attention. Let's face it, this is the internet age. Many home buyers will go online well before they start working with a realtor, and get a good idea of the homes they want to see. This is why getting a dominant web presence is important to a realtor or director. Another important aspect of the home promotion that an agent excels about is getting access to other agents. This is one of the most critical steps in the process of home sales. Typically an agent can build working relationships with community consumer agent groups and host realtor-exclusive shows where the home can be shown to all agents in your town/city. The results of this are, as you can guess, enormous. A realtor also has an operating budget in place to secure print and media advertising. This should include full-page colour ads in the local newspaper, and posters on the sign in your front yard accessible 24 hours a day. Without help from realtors, this kind of coverage is almost impossible to gain.

A realtor is spending energy, attention, and resources in your property when it comes to selling your house. Knowing that the house is being marketed promptly and at the lowest price available is in their own interest. You will highlight the house in a way other homeowners are unable to do due to the time involved. We have greater exposure to communications channels and have extensive business awareness. You may be shocked to ask your realtor what they are doing to sell a home properly.

Technology is quickly on the run. This forms the way we work. Revolutionizing the way we connect and interact. There's very nothing that was unaffected by development. Industries were razed, and new ones almost immediately were erected in their absence. Company titans have fallen and folded into the paws of technology. Blockbuster Sound. "Toys R Us. Kodak. Kodak. Google. Google. Microsoft-Nokia. Xerox-Xerox. Terms that once represented something are now lost into thin air.

Today they have been succeeded by businesses such as Uber, Netflix, Amazon, Facebook and others leading the way in the midst of modern age. They embrace change; they reshape and disrupt business as we know it. However, one sector has been left relatively unscathed despite all the innovations and all the transition. Immovable Properties. The truth is selling your house in this country is still such an antiquated process. It is an outdated concept focused on. Another that depends on infinite frictional selection.

Could you sell your property now fast? This depends on a fast description of yourself. Is it as fast as ordering an Uber or renting a holiday apartment on Airbnb? Heck it out no. Can you sell your house on a platform like Lending Tree as fast as you would get a mortgage to purchase a new one? NOTHING. You can't sell it so fast by any measure unless you want to put your home out there on a fire sale for pennies on the dollar. You have to run over obstacles and barriers today. Interminable miles of red tape. Staff. Committees. And payments which are never-ending. Such is the standard. The exception is not so.

Like travel, trade and culture, real estate has evolved gradually. The legalities are infinite, and the complications. There are, of course, faster ways to sell your home. They include heading to businesses which we label iBuyers. Meaning, they themselves purchase the commodity. Organizations such as OpenDoor, OfferPad and even Zillow have all jumped into the ring. And appropriately so. But is that helping you to get the top dollar as you market it directly? Completely not.

How to sell your house fast

Anyone who knows me knows I am technologically obsessed. As an engineer, I dump bits and bytes and bend and prod them to my will. I spend countless hours crafting smart code. Then there will be even more testing and optimisation. So I have been working to fix the question for the last two years. It's a really big issue. The problem is, how do you build a website and a forum to offer your home at a quick pace and yet get top dollar? And how do you do all this without actually using an immovable agent to navigate the whole process?

This was the origin of Kribbz, the real estate firm that I have been developing over the past few years. It's a network that utilizes the blockchain, the fastest and cheapest method to store evidence — purchases are unchangeable and unchallenged. My dream in the immediate future is that it would remove the need to fork over a 6 per cent real estate fee just to sell the house.

Yet there are other options to sell your home quick now, right here and right now. No, it's not fast because we are creating a website. This is a little bit quicker. And if you are playing the hypothetical cards correctly, you will use strategies and tactics to achieve the best bang for the so-called dollar. Again everything depends on your quick definition. Could you sell the house as fast as you can order the Uber? At least not anymore. But you can sell it easily, moderately. Ok, here's how.

Understanding the mechanics of home selling

There are some aspects that can't easily be modified when it comes to selling your house. Such affect the velocity of selling. They 're sort of place stuff. You listen like it all the way. Place, location, place. If your home is situated in a particularly desirable area or right on the shore, you 're definitely in luck. Quite definitely it would move fast. Business dynamics too. Is there a competition for sellers? Or is it a demand for buyers? You can't change that really apart from waiting for it out. But you're never sure how long each one will last.

And how long does a property usually take to sell? The nationwide average amount of days a house stays on the market is 68 days according to Zillow Report. This, of course, depends on the place, and whether it is the business of a seller or buyer. But it depends on the size, as well. When you are hunting for the highest dollar, stay now. So, don't demand high dollar if your house is in bad shape. For examples, Zillow says homes in Palo Alto, CA was on the market for an average of 36 days. Illinois at Peoria? 136 Years.

Dave Grandone

1. Sell your house to a wholesaler

What most people don't realize is that almost 40 per cent of all real estate transactions happen in this country, use all the currency. That means banks do not participate. This also indicates the bulk of the conventional underwriting barriers are gone. Yet wholesalers are doing something even more special. They 're supporting your room, middle guy, just for the Upper Dollar. But you are going to get a decent sum. This is for sure. On their end, they have lined up cash customers who inform them what product they are involved in.

All that the wholesaler does is sell the house and transfer it to a cash bidder. That also requires little to no money out of their wallet. Then why do you turn it back to a wholesaler? Well, this is easy. Surely speedier than having to mention it with a conventional seller. Here, how can you come across a wholesaler? This is a little bit more complex. Still, they consider you. We search for indications in their hunt for troubled sellers whose assets are willing to sell at a deep discount.

So what are you going to do if you don't want to expect them to find you? Using one of WeBuyUglyHouses, or some of the other regional companies out there. Yet keep in mind that you are likely to offer the commodity to the dollar at 60 to 70 cents. Other ways to source wholesalers on your own is to search for something like "sell a house for cash" on Google, followed by the name of your state or town. You may also check for "cash buyers real estate" or other related words and use Facebook Groups or LinkedIn and access cash buyers.

2. Find the best real estate agent in your area.

All correct. There is a major difference that I have to stress among real estate agents here. While I personally have nothing against them, here's the fact. Some of the workers had positive ideas. Surely they have every plan to sell your house for top dollar. So they want to start selling it soon. But normally, is that the case? Not too much. Many complain that the realtors are not doing their job yet. The entire issue about list-it-and-forget-it appears to be taking centre stage. And very reasonably so. At the end of the day, you give up 6 per cent of your home price.

There are 2 million registered real estate brokers in the United States. Among which about 1.35 million are accredited, officers, according to the American Realtors Association. But, still, a very limited number of such approved agents earn profits. And the more they're agents, the greater their chances of being high earners. Throughout the years, and over time, you build partnerships with your company balloons. And if you decide to sell fast, those are the agents you want to go to.

And how do you come across a top real estate agent in your area? Only. Easy. Only do the web scanning. Something like "best Los Angeles real estate agent" or whatever area you 're in. Look for the hundreds of positive reviews from realtors. Find the top growers, and see if they're going to list your house. Will that suggest you 're trying to market them overnight? Never not. So the strongest shot you have at pushing the property quicker than the average in your field is to go with a high performer who has already formed relationships.

3. Cutting down the quality drastically.

See, you really can't change your home place. You really couldn't. But the price will change. And based on the market environment, the cycle may be significantly escalated by increasing the price drastically. I am not asking about a tiny market change. I am talking about a major asking price change. When you're priced at $400,000, bringing that down to $350,000 is a drastic price shift. Dropping it down by $5,000 here won't give you well.

What more would want to do is delete and relist the home from the MLS again. That's all well and good, but the property has a past made. Everyone will see how many days he invested in the market. They'll always learn whether you're a good dealer or not. Rather than taking it off the shelf and relisting it, just lower the price. Price is an immense motivating factor, once again. Keep in mind that at a drastic discount, people love stuff.

Remember, be mindful that the property has to be substantial relative to other neighbourhood properties. When you lowered the price significantly and are still expensive compared to the other houses, it won't make a difference. People want a really great deal. They 'd rather purchase a neighbourhood's least expensive house than the most expensive. For certain people, all the enhancements might be significant. But if you decide to move fast, this mainly involves the size.

4. Find a fast house deal.

If customers try to move fast, that is mainly because they are underwater. These properties are what we call distressed. Why? For what? As the mortgage due to the house is always higher than the home 's worth. This implies wealth is inexistent. Plus, it aggravates the problem when you go through a breakup, a spouse's death, or bankruptcy, among other financial problems. So when you don't have any further money to cover the lease, that's when you start losing your house absolutely.

It is not a very good situation. So if you've been hit with bankruptcy by the government, there is stuff you should consider. The most notable? Tell the bank to make a short sale. Which sort of a fast sale? Secondly, it depends on the mortgage being higher than the home valuation. But it still depends on the consent of all lien holders to the transaction. And if you've got three lenders, they all ought to decide on a short sale. When you have one, the odds of short selling your home are obviously higher.

How do you do it? You need to call the holder of the primary note. That's the largest holder of the home mortgages. If you have only one mortgage, that's fine. Contact the Branch. Ask them what the case is like. And figure out about what you need to talk to get out of underwater. Indeed, this is both awkward and degrading. But that is definitely better than a foreclosure. It's safer than getting your own house evicted.

5. Transfer your mortgage to another individual.

Sure, the last option to easily sell your house could be to move your mortgage over to someone else. Yet that still ensures that everyone else needs to take the mortgage for granted. To find this out, you may need to consult your mortgage papers. Yet if that's supposable, you 're in luck. It may also mean you will live and let it in your house. Was that a typical scenario? No. And it may be. You just have to do some research with the legs to make things possible.

Bear in mind that whosoever is the current "borrower," they must apply for the mortgage. So it might require a few hurdles to go through. And if you're really buried under debt and can't make your payments, it's probably not the fastest way to get out of your home. But they're an alternative. How long does it take for this? This all depends, again. Contact your bank and see if even that is a thing. If it is, then you would still need to locate the person who is able to take over the mortgage first.

How To Effectively Market Your House

It becomes easier to market your home if you are able to identify the current real estate market. Agents prefer to expend a lot of time and focus on sales listings as markets switch from seller's to buyer's markets, but good marketing tactics are just sound business sense regardless. Some homes scream out for drone imaging, particularly if they're situated on the coast, in the woods, in a lake, or on broad grounds. In such situations, an aerial perspective will be a major asset for highlighting the local area.

A night view of the home illuminated by outside lighting is another important feature that is frequently used in luxury home marketing.

Effective selling in a seller's market may offer better costs, so it may be the difference between "produced" or "expired" in a buyer's market. Effective publicity might not sell the home, but it will make the phone ring so you won't sell if customers don't call.

Photograph the Front

Most homebuyers begin a home search online so posting good photos is essential. Listings without photos or with only an exterior shot are often ignored. But that doesn't mean an exterior shot from the front isn't very important.

Your house photo will look ten times better than your competition's if you crop out sidewalks and streets. Remove vehicles from your driveway and from the front of your home. Shoot both closes up and angled photos and avoid shade falling on the house — wait for another time of day if necessary.

Clear away any vegetation that's blocking the front door or the path to the door.

Other Exterior Photographs

So if you own an apartment or townhome with no yard, take photos of the clubhouse, lawn, gym, or tennis courts. But keep in mind that if you do have a yard, buyers will want to see it.

Emphasize space and take a long shot. Rip down the grass and cut the trees. Delete some proof of pets and put away the toys for babies. Stop taking shot in the heat.

Interior Photographs

Take photos of each room, particularly though you think a particular space isn't going to photograph well. Shoot it anyway, because you might simply be surprised by the photo quality. It may be available.

Open blinds then drape, then switch the lights on. Focus on interesting details such as a wood floor condition, or a fireplace mantle. Drop garbage bins and cover bathroom toilet lids, and use flower decorations in kitchens and dining areas.

Consider firing into the mirrors as it will represent your image.

Virtual Tours

Virtual tours are no longer just for families with a million-dollar exhibit. Every home should have one, even though these are just two spins. Buyers enjoy virtual tours, feeling love.

A good virtual tour, whether it's 360 or a video, will grab a buyer by the hand and lead her from room to room. You may incorporate visual, music, or an entertaining, professionally written summary that scrolls along with the tour 's progress, depending on the tour operator.

Digital tours can also provide individual images which can be accessed or printed.

Signage

Signage invites home shoppers to contact you, or your partner, instantly. This is commercial-free! A well-designed "For Sale" sign generates phone calls. If your home is in a corner space, put up two signs.

Keep in mind that property signs are prohibited by some homeowner's associations. They just require signs from windows.

Attempt to speak to a neighbour whose house is situated at the corner of a busy street, requesting for approval to put a sign with an arrow pointing to yours in that yard.

If the agency has several branches, agent signs will contain the phone number of their nearest location. They should include the cellphone number of the agent, as well.

Print Advertising

Magazine advertisements hit consumers reading newspapers and receiving web ads to others. When the neighbours claim, "I see the home advertising everywhere I turn!" you are doing a nice job.

Ads placed in major newspapers. Check out which days more writers are moving along. It's normally Sunday, but on some days, even several newspapers post "photo classifieds."

Don't skip the nearby newspapers. With less capital, you may also run a wider ad that matches more specifically those that are searching in your particular region.

Before putting advertisements in real estate magazines, test the press dates. Eventually, make use of any page you can access, as most internet directories are free of charge.

Direct Mail

If you're an unrepresented vendor, you should purchase mailing lists from the email brokers when you're served by an agent talk for a direct mail system. Oversized four-colour postcards are perfect because they are cheap and eye-catching to send. Give some to your neighbours. Everyone has friends and relatives who may wish to move close to them.

Offer them to brokers in your community that serve sellers, both to sellers that reside in other places and also move to your community.

Open Houses

Because of its position or other reasons, not every home is ideal for an open house, but often the best way to find out is to attempt. When no one arrives, that is usually a positive sign.

If your home is near a high-traffic region where customers often flock, this is potentially a successful choice. Put open house signs all over the region, guiding purchasers to your place. Advertise the newspaper open house, and publish electronic open house dates.

(Do not hesitate to call the neighbours, they will arrive anyway.)

Host Broker/Agent Tours

If you intend on selling your home without advertising, you may bypass this phase, but it's a good idea to get as many agents and brokers as possible to see your house. Some of the customers have officers.

Agents that stay in your home can help recall information to explain to customers later on, so food is the perfect way to entice an agent to stick around. It doesn't have to be expensive, anything. Sandwiches will be plenty. The idea is they would enjoy your home while they munch and network, and then put a customer out

Send E-Flyers

Technology makes electronic flyers very simple to manufacture and deliver. You should take many pictures of your home. Costs vary, but usually, they are not prohibitively costly to manufacture.

Give them to real estate agents who sell in your city, as well as relatives, family and colleagues. It may also be goals for out-of-town brokers and agents that serve customers in your market.

PRICING YOUR HOME AT THE PERFECT PRICE

W here ever you glance, there are houses up for rent in any neighbourhood; When you decide to sell your house fast, and you intend to sell it, what will you do? Well, you have to be mindful of two crucial things, time and resources.

You are in the best position because you have plenty of room and use all the resources available. This will allow you to sell your property exactly where it needs to be, and then you can just wait to see the right buyer. You have to wait for the right customer all the time, so you don't need to be versatile about the prices.

There appears to be a lot of such assets on the market at the moment. That has contributed to huge inventories of homes now on offer. Many of these properties are actually overpriced for the business, however, if the investors are willing to wait, consumer demand may finally catch up with them.

The part of the vendors is individuals under a time rush and a capital pinch right now. An indication of that being someone who has a new house constructed, or who has just bought a new, used house with a closing date quickly approaching. Such citizens are left with the dilemma of charging two mortgages, one on an empty building. And even still, a number of people use the funds from the first property selling to purchase the new home.

It will place an immense strain on a family because if they focus a latest investment six months earlier on the valuation of a house, they may find themselves short of funds. Homes in certain places have dropped as much as 50 per cent below their high point, which is nevertheless considered to be a major deviation below homeowners hopes.

Even if they are selling their correctly at the correct amount they need to deliver fast, they have to make the difference out of their own assets or risk the threat of defaulting on the other sales deal. This can be quite a risky situation for a homeowner when they try to create a perfect price for their land. They ought to be only a little below the valuation of equivalent property so that they gain the most interest and can, therefore, secure a shorter closing time. But they can't be too small because they can't handle their latest real estate.

Finally, there are people who have issues with time and are not worried about the earnings. Such individuals have usually built up quite a bit of money, and are selling because of family circumstances or work opportunities. Moving quickly is more relevant than making the most revenue possible. For their prices and whatever conditions the customer wants, they are very versatile, as long as they have a very quick closing date.

Based on the time constraint, either these vendors are very actively selling their property, or they approach several of the numerous fast buy companies out there that will purchase properties quickly but need cheaper rates to make it worth it.

Pricing Your Home To Sell

The single most critical thing to remember when selling a house is that you have correctly priced it.

You have to choose the best price tag depending on how much your property is worth if you decide to sell it.

The Pricing Dilemma

You don't want to overprice the house so within the first two or three weeks of showings you may ruin the freshness of the attraction of the estate. Demand and concern waned after around 21 days. Of example, nothing keeps you from lowering the price later, but it may be too-little-too-late.

On the other side, don't think about selling something too low, because homes priced below market value are also offered several deals. This will drive the price to market afterwards. Pricing is all about demand and availability. It is part beauty of art and part technology.

No two agents have similarly priced properties. Many brokers are far better at working out how to sell your house than most, so others can perform a great deal of this job for you and do a comprehensive study of the competition in advance. Those are the basic elements of the method.

Pull Comparable Listings and Sales

Check at any comparable home that has been reported in the same area in the last three months as your house. Appraisers don't use comps for longer than three months.

The list should be limited to homes within 1/4 mile to a radius of 1/2 mile unless there is only a handful of comps in the general rural vicinity of the property.

Be careful about dividing neighbourhood lines and physical barriers such as major streets, freeways or railroads. Don't equate product from the "other side of the tracks." In some areas, similar homes directly across the street may differ by as much as $100,000. Perceptions have meaning and desirability.

Where appropriate, equate equivalent square footage within a range of 10 per cent up or down. Connect equivalent years. One community may consist of homes from the 1980s that were constructed in the 1950s right next to another building ring. Words vary from the two. Verify you equate apples with oranges.

Honestly, appraise desirability. If you're lucky enough to have a dream home that will render buyers slow when you join, you could get away with a luxury tacking.

Check out the Sold Comps

Now associate initial list prices with actual sale rates to assess price changes. To calculate the percentages, equate the overall list prices to the real sales rates. It is normal for homes to sell on the market of a seller for more than 100 per cent of the list price. Homes typically sell at a purchaser's rate for list price or less.

Change prices for variances in lot scale, design, and facilities or enhancements.

Withdrawn and Expired Listings

Pull the background on any removed and disabled listings to decide whether all of them have been taken off the market and relisted. If not, apply certain days on the market back to certain time spans for advertising to arrive at a real amount of days on the market.

Look for trends as to why such homes have not sold and take care of the similar reasons they that share. Whose brokerage was on the listing? Is it a firm that regularly sells all it listed, or was it a discount brokerage that may not have invested enough time on the home marketing?

Pending Sales

Such homes' final sale rates are undisclosed before the end of the sale, but that doesn't deter you from contacting the advertising agents and telling them to inform you how much the house sells for. Any agents are going to. Any do not.

Take notice of the days at the market again. This will have a strong impact on how long it would take to see a bid. To assess price cuts, analyze the context of such listings.

Active Listings

Know sellers will ask anything they want. It doesn't mean they are going to get this amount. Tour these active-listing properties, and when they come, you will see what customers can do. Take care of what you enjoy and hate, and of the overall impression that you have when you reach the homes, when necessary, replicate the pleasant welcome experiences in your own house.

Those assets are your match. Ask yourself why a customer should choose your home and change the price accordingly.

Square Foot Cost Comparisons

When you accept a bid, the buyer's lender can request an assessment, and you'll want to equate homes with comparable square footage and get as near as possible to the final appraised valuation. Appraisers do not want to deviate more than 25% and tend to stick under 10 % of total square footage computations when the house is 2,000 square feet, so equivalent homes are 1,800 to 2,200 square feet.

Average square foot expense does not suggest you can easily subtract by that amount your square feet, at least not when your home is of average scale. The price per square foot reduces as the scale declines, and the value rises. Larger homes cost fewer square foot, while smaller homes cost square foot.

Market Dependent Pricing

The next move, once you have compiled all the data, is to interpret the data depending on business conditions. Let's assume the last three equivalent purchases in your area is $250,000, for comparative purposes.

Your purchase price will allow some wiggle room in a buyer's market for bargaining. However, you'll want to be high enough and near enough to the last comparable selling to draw a buyer to visit your house. You will expect to pay $249,900 for your house and opt for $245,000 to sell in this sector. You would want to pay up to the last equivalent selling in the business of a retailer 10 per cent higher. You should pay more than the last equivalent offer, so if there is no inventory and a ton of customers, you'll usually get it. The $250,000 house could be going for $265,000 or more.

You may want to initially set the price at the last comparable offer on a healthy or stable sector, then change it to the current pattern. If the last transaction comes to a close three months earlier, but since then the median price has risen more than 1 per cent every month, it will make sense to sell at $254,500.

How to Sell Your Home for the Highest Price

Once you've agreed to sell your home, you may be tempted only to place it on the market right away and see whether someone is willing to give you a bid "as it is." It used to be that prospective investors can see past the nature of the surface to "see the possibilities." With little to no fixes to cosmetics needed, buyers today want to move in.

"So may somebody's going to make a bid to me," you say. "Why do I intend to lose?"

The danger that you're performing 20 shows and you do not have any deals. News spreads out inside the realtor culture like flames. It is impossible to come back from a first encounter that is negative.

Until bringing it on the market, the most popular realtors would advise you to keep your house in good shape. There are lots of information to accomplish this aim, and we have defined five main fields. We're calling them "C's 5."

1. Clutter

2. Cleaning

3. Cosmetics

4. Curb Appeal

5. Communications

Clutter

There's no grace on potential customers. It all sticks out like a sore thumb for them. Although you can consider slight imperfections trivial, they may be a deal-breaker.

Clutter is the first to tackle a squeaky egg. When your wardrobes are loaded, your rooms overfilled, your storage areas cramped, you need to move stuff out of the house and into storage. The effect would be a more open and viable look and sound. There is a range of businesses that can sell off plastic bins called "Pods." You prepare it, they pick it up and store it, and distribute it anywhere you want it. In an 8′ x 8′ by 16′ tub, the total period of time it takes to restore a house and rent it costs around $1,300 in six months of storage.

The uncluttering phase is indeed a perfect excuse to throw unused things out. Many products at Goodwill Industries can be dropped off to are a tax write-off. Among other stuff, an 8′ x 8′ x 7′ dumpster costs about $400. Many people tend to underestimate the size of dumpster they want, and on the high side, they misinterpret.

Most realtors deal for a "stager" as a final step, who will help you organize the home items the most enticing way. Some stagers have mobilization warehouses to boost the overall performance.

Cleaning

Prospective customers are finding ashes, scratches and smudges in a sitcom series like the finicky mother-in-law. Some blemish is just another excuse to fall in love with your house. Also, if you employ a qualified cleaning company, with a spray bottle and paper towel in hand, you can walk the building.

The Best Homes & Gardens website is a clear source of knowledge for some kind of cleaning

One of the first items people say in your house is the floors. These future deal breakers contain wallpaper streaks, wood surface blemishes, concrete flaws or linoleum. Ideally, sweeping is a solution, but you may need to remove floor coverings in certain situations, polish wood floors, and repaint walls and woodwork.

Washing carpets is usually achieved by specialists who use steam cleaning machines at a rate of about 50 cents a square foot. Follow the cycle many times while you use a carpet vacuum until the water in the bucket is dirt clear. Second, sweep for hardwood floors, then scrub with a moist cloth that includes a solvent for washing wood flooring. Whether the oils have reached the surface, they must be cleaned and sanded.

Within and outside, equipment should be properly washed. Using a degreasing solvent on kitchen equipment, exhaust fan grates and kitchen surfaces.

Cosmetics

"Cosmetics" involves offering bare surfaces a fresh look and sound. It ensures that floor coverings, wood floors, ceilings, woodwork, furniture and appliances are washed, repainted or repaired. You re-surface what you can't clean. You remove that much you can't resurface. You restructure or replace what looks old and dated.

If your carpet is over five years old, you should probably replace it at 2013 prices at the cost of around $3 per square foot. (We are replacing any carpet older than two years). Refinishing hardwood floors cost around $4.50 a foot, and repairing about $6.00 a foot. Fresh linoleum and tile cost around the same as ï¿½1⁄2- $3 a square foot carpeting. With fresh parts from the system supplier, models will be rendered to appear brand new. This will render a stove look squeaky clean with fresh burners, grates and drip pans. When you have outdated or obsolete appliances, you might find new appliances. A new refrigerator, fridge, dishwasher, and microwave would cost around $2,000, so it will help you earn an additional $5,000 for the property and make you market it more easily.

A dark, dank basement can be a deal-breaker as well. Whether the walls contain soil, water movement or mould, it helps to wipe them off and add two coats of white paint blocking water. This often rising pollution and odours. Likewise, the surface may be completely converted by first cleaning and then adding two epoxy paint coats.

You get to sell your house quicker at a better price with an expenditure of $200.

Curb Appeal

The theory goes you just have one chance to make a successful first impression. An unattractive exterior will affect the way the consumer perceives the interior. A beautiful look and sound outside make the potential more accommodating for what they see inside.

Studies have found 40 per cent of your curb value is your building. If it is soiled or discoloured a perfectly good roof can look like it needs replacement. Get it washed professionally for about $300 and the roof problem is gone. Be sure they use low-pressure nozzles and products licensed by EPA that won't harm your greenery. Most roofers can also fuel the sidewalls and windows while at it.

A lawn infested with weeds may be a turn off too. With a $30 spray tank and a $12 weed killer pump, you'll be ready to rid your weed lawn in a few weeks. The easiest approach to green up the lawn is then with granulated fertilizer that feeds in a time-release manner over liquids that just produce a short-lived green light. You should cut the shrubbery back, so it doesn't get an overgrown or overlooked feel. In certain instances, shrubbery that appears aged or unsightly is best discarded and substituted with new plantings.

If you do not scrub up the siding and trim with power washing or other devices, you may need to get it repainted. This can cost from $2,000 to $5,000, depending on the size of the house, but you will usually recoup it at a higher selling price.

Communications

The primary source of communications for houses on the market is the MLS web site that is only accessible by realtors. If you are attempting to sell your house without a realtor, the location where nearly all of them go for listings is absent. Many major real estate companies often have their own platform where the MLS database shows any home. Most pages which have titles such as "House Hunt" are labelled as realtor pages.

All this suggests is that you would consider it very tough to sell the house without charging 6 per cent realtor fee. Many realtors are likely to work harder than some to sell the house though. Choose one that provides value-added facilities such as skilled photographers providing the lenses and equipment to render the images as beautiful as possible. Search for realtors that carry in "stagers" full of decorated warehouses to improve the look and sound of your home. We advocate not engaging in something that goes beyond pleasing images and explanations. Buyers don't want videos as they tend to swipe on the images they want to view immediately, instead of waiting for the video to get there.

Ensure sure your house achieves what your communications say, in all communications. Showings sometimes amount to frustration.

The Sixth C - Compromise

There's a sixth "C" we didn't inform you about ï¿1/2- Compromise. Which is, you can already have to fall down in quality until you totally cover all the 5 "Cs." There have been so many times where sellers refuse a decent deal out of modesty or obstinacy, only to be compelled to consider a lower bid eventually.

Dave Grandone

FINANCING REAL ESTATE INVESTMENT

Many of us approach property investing, financing it with a credit report or lendings from a bank. Yet the truth about getting into this area is that when obtaining involved with real estate investing, financing it making use of credit report can really be unneeded, as well as using financings, and also any type of ventures with any kind of and all banks simply aren't needed in all. The main ingredient to establishing this prowess of smooth and also unconfined real estate investing, funding everything with no of these, is certainly, knowledge.

To accomplish this does not take mere "pointers as well as methods" that are just workable in isolated circumstances, or if the scenarios are just right ... there actually exist strategies of dealing with property investing without funding it with these typical means. Excellent credit or bad, it really needn't enter into the picture whatsoever. Banks and fundings can really be a hindrance in many scenarios, so to heck with them.

Furthermore, using these techniques aren't just exercised by those who just can't do it otherwise, such as those with little or no funding, but by the most effective investors in property, for whom the usual extra ways of financing their ventures are no worry in any way. Sure, they could go through the process of realty investing, financing it using these usual facilities, yet if things could be done far quicker as well as extra effectively without them, then really, why trouble? Like the claiming goes, "Job smarter, not harder". These "underground strategies" are the very best means to come close to property investing, funding it without a credit report, financial institutions or loans, or perhaps with almost no funding.

'The Property Underground' Is a detailed plan to success when buying a property even if you have no money and an inadequate credit report ranking.

Funding real estate investments are extremely crucial for any building capitalist. Several lending institutions are much happier to supply financial investment lendings since they can include your estimate earnings to your finance application. If you need funds for your new investment, there are a variety of ways that you can create what you need.

The first option is to go with a regular financial institution mortgage. Financial institutions do lend cash for investments as well as typical mortgages, though you may find that your options are slightly different from a traditional home mortgage. It helps if you have an excellent credit rating. If so, you will be able to locate car loans with a reduced interest rate. It helps to search in order to locate the terms that function most in your favour.

The next choice for you is to select a private financier. These are people who have cash money available yet don't intend to make the investment themselves. You would require to find a shared contract and also let them recognize the information of the financial investment. They will additionally require proof to show that it's most likely to pay off if they're most likely to take the risk of offering the money. It is an excellent concept to have a solicitor prepare an agreement in this circumstance!

Finally, you could try a hard money lender for your investment, though this ought to only be a short term option as the passion is normally billed at a really high rate. Take some time to compare and discover what type of financing for real estate investments are readily available to you on the best terms.

Property Spending Using Exclusive Money Car Loans - The Ultimate Win-Win Situation

If you are like a most starting investor, the primary roadblock you face as you get going is getting the money you require to money your bargains. Many individuals have difficulty thinking beyond the package and also coming up with innovative ways to fund their properties. With strict certifying standards, lots of limitations, as well as large down payments, a lot of financiers don't have the methods needed to obtain finance from a typical financial institution. The good news is, there are other techniques you can use to fund your realty transactions, the very best being private cash. Using personal cash permits financiers to act quicker on possible offers allowing them to defeat the competitors and also aid numerous distressed homeowners by taking trouble residential property off their hands.

Dave Grandone

What is Exclusive Money?

Exclusive money is a very common term utilized by the act of providing cash to an investor by a personal individual. When a personal cash loan is made, residential property is bought and also the loan provider obtains a first or bank loan or deed of trust (depending upon your state) on that home, securing their legal rate of interest. After the acquisition, the real estate investor will certainly then use the rest of the loan to refurbish and also sell that certain home. These car loans will certainly always be made on a reduced Loan-to-Value ratio, normally 75% or much less, which boosts the safety and security of the investment. For instance, if a home is valued at $100,000, a private lender would certainly never lend more than $75,000 on that particular property. After the improvements have actually been total and also the building marketed, the private lending institution will be repaid the principal of the finance plus passion made established by the previously agreed upon rate.

The Investor

Making use of private money fundings is the single best method to fund the growth of any realty investing business. The benefits of using exclusive cash can not be matched by any other kind of innovative funding. The number one factor that utilizing personal cash is such a benefit to real estate investors is since it improves the residential or commercial property buying process, enabling even more transactions to be finished faster, causing raised earnings. Being able to use a quick closing with cash money provided by exclusive lenders will inspire vendors to take your offer over the competition. This will certainly likewise attract them to take a much-reduced cost than they would certainly from a traditional purchaser. Also, considering that investor discovers as well as purchase properties up until now listed below market value, these exclusive loans typically cover 100% of the purchase cost as well as some or every one of the renovation prices. Additionally, without a down payment, and also many times no month-to-month payment on the lending, it's very easy to see why this technique is the number one technique for funding property investment bargains. Considering that making use of personal cash is such an advantage to an investor, they want to use lending institutions high-interest rates.

The Exclusive Lender

So why should individuals select exclusive financing over even more typical investments such as the stock market? Well, the solution is basic: even more control, higher yields, and also little danger. When you selected to be a private loan provider, you control the terms of your financial investment, choose the size of your term, your interest rate, and also when you receive settlements. Depending on each certain investment, you can choose to provide funds anywhere from a few days up to 5 years. An investor using personal fundings often times will certainly provide yields that are much more than virtually any other investment lorry, commonly earning anywhere from 8%-12% as well as in some cases as much as 15%. You chose when to receive passion settlements whether it be monthly, quarterly, each year or at the time of car loan maturation. The threat is reduced with a cosigned promissory note providing your security, an act of trust or home loan safeguarding your legal passion, and also an insurance policy securing you from accidents. There are many different sources personal lenders can utilize to take advantage of this sort of investment. With the capacity to utilize cash money, an Individual Retirement Account, 401k, home equity, bank card and even more, personal borrowing with real estate investors is an extraordinary financial investment possibility. High fixed returns secured by real properties, insured versus crashes, with the capability to be totally tax-free within your retirement account.

Variety is a very crucial part of any kind of financial investment profile. With the advantages exclusive lending gives incorporated with the volatility of other extra conventional financial investments like the existing stock exchange, there could not be a far better time than now to explore this sort of investing. So what are you waiting on?

Property Spending - Factors to Determine If You Are Ready to Safeguarding Realty Funding

Financial investment in property indicates purchasing dealt with assets, especially in buildings. Realty financial investment is a rewarding business having a variety of possibilities for making good money. But financial investment must be carried out only after acquiring a complete understanding of the business and also mastering the techniques of the trade. If you intend to be a real estate investor, you must discover methods of protecting money for your bargains. This is the first and also the primary step in the business, given that, without financing, you can not take the following action.

Getting financing for real estate is not as very easy as it utilized to be in the past. Its reason being the present economic crisis and also the following risks that are encountered by the loan provider.

Listed below, we review some aspects that can aid you to protect a realty funding facility with family member ease as well as comfort. We will assess the result of the current financial slowdown, methods which loan provider has changed their borrowing procedures, as well as how you can quickly adapt to their existing disposition.

Credit score merit

Whenever you obtain funding, the first thing the lender will certainly demand to understand is your credit scores worthiness. He will certainly validate your earnings as well as likewise inspect whether you are already servicing funding. If you are strained with a couple of financings, he will certainly hesitate to offer you an additional. The most basic principle governing credit rating merit of a potential customer is very easy: He or she has to have the capacity to pay off the funding.

Place of the building

The following point your lender will certainly try to find is the location of the residential property in which you are preparing to spend. If the building has a high market value, it will translate into bigger profits for you as well as strengthen your capability to settle the lending. On the other hand, if the property has no market value, it will certainly place you in a jam as well as you can end up being incapable of servicing the funding. Aside from the location of the residential or commercial property, the lender will also consider other aspects that could impact your future productivity. They include the dimension as well as the problem of the residential or commercial property and the cost you intend to spend for it.

Risk Factor

The default of a client is the timeless concern of the lending institution. There are numerous factors that might finish in default. You should guarantee the lender that no such thing will certainly occur to the funding provided to you. For this purpose, you can present them with your previous debt servicing document. You should additionally make sure and convince the lending institution that there are no danger factors associated with the property that you intend to purchase.

Select the best lending institution

The lender is one of the most important people in your realty venture, so it is imperative that you pick the best one. The lending institution needs to want to fund you as well as you ought to really feel comfortable taking care of him. You must, on your part, be very honest as well as co-operative. Several of the questions asked - as well as records required- by the lending institution, seem irritating. They are not. He is just examining things out and ensuring that the centre that he encompasses you is a great and also safe and secure investment.

If you have finished all the documentation beforehand, and also are willing to co-operate with the lender, there is no reason that you must fall short to get a feasible financing centre for your property deal.

Property Investing Boils Down to Money, Evaluations, and also Calculations

An audio understanding of money, appraisals, and also estimations is required for successful real estate investing. It goes without saying, that anyone who has actually had property investment success has needed to rely upon their understanding of the important components of value such as how to calculate capital, revenue taxes, market pressures, funding, as well as financial investment accept make it with financial investment realty.

Finance

Since most financiers finance a major part of the purchase price, you require to recognize is that your genuine expense is not the sale of the home but the total you pay over the years. As well as this is just one of the most vital questions investors ask due to the fact that investors require to recognize how much their financial investments need in resources.

For example, if you purchase a rental property for $300,000, put $90,000 down, as well as finance the equilibrium of $210,000 for three decades at 7.5%, you would end up paying a whole lot much more in passion than you would certainly with a similar car loan at a 6.0% interest rate.

To put it simply, at the end of the day, maybe a mistake if you focus mostly on the price of a home with little regard for the very best home mortgage offer and the outcomes of substance interest.

Valuation

Rental properties differ considerably in expense as well as in high quality, place, and revenue possibility. It do without stating as a result that sound realty investing depends on the study and also evaluation of each one of those factors together with the termination of a couple of misconceptions: particularly, that property worths always increase, revenue over the long-term is the most crucial requirement, as well as you can't lose with real estate.

In reality, the realty market moves in cycles (both backwards and forwards), you always need to worry on your own with the capital (not merely the long-term profit), so you can be sure that the property generates adequate income to cover the mortgage payments and overhead during your holding duration, as well as unless you research your neighbourhood market beforehand in an intelligent manner, you can endure losses on your financial investment.

The concept is to concentrate your valuation on your details market using suitable information bordering the type of building you are most thinking about purchasing. To put it simply, regardless of regional and also nationwide fads you have to come down to the market supply as well as need elements right in your town (all patterns are neighbourhood). Moreover, if your realty spending purpose is to invest in multifamily units don't obtain shut off because the real estate market is down. The supply as well as need cycles for own a home and for rentals stand out and separate.

Computations

The estimations needed for financiers to evaluate the outcomes between properties, to set minimum standards, or to compare rates of return in between realty and also other sorts of investment are normally critical to financiers.

Realty investing, nevertheless, is constantly concerning the bottom line. Whereas you would want to know exactly how the home's capitalization price contrasts to other comparable buildings in the area prior to your acquisition, how much (before and also after-tax) cash flow you can expect to get during a particular holding period and also how much tax obligation shelter you may benefit from, of a special rate of interest to the investor is their return on investment as well as how it compares in between making a financial investment in real estate to various other sorts of investments such as interest-bearing accounts, mutual funds, or stocks that could be extra rewarding to the investor.

Get Control of Your Finances Prior To You Begining Realty Spending

If you are sliding further and even more right into financial obligation monthly and also you believe realty investing is going to save you, I have trouble for you. It will not. Let me inform you first hand that if those testimonials on late night t.v. for no cash down training courses are also real, those individuals are the exemption, not the rule. That's the trouble - fortunately, is that there are lower-danger means to acquire property as well as you don't need to have money to do it.

From a lot of disappointments making no money down bargains, I have actually come to the verdict that newbie real estate investors should prevent 100% financing on residential or commercial property purchases. They are really dangerous as well as while there are individuals that I've gotten really abundant doing them, there are probably a lot more than shed a great deal of cash. That's what occurred to me as well as, no money deals still cost money! It simply indicates you do not have to spend cash on a deposit.

In my sight, there are only three methods you need to take into consideration developing a down payment to begin realty investing. However, the bright side is that just one of them calls for that you to use your own cash:

1. Your own financial savings (cash out supplies, GIC's, and even retirement savings in some cases).

2. Equity in your house.

3. A partner with cash money.

Notice charge card and also credit lines are not on that checklist?! DO NOT USE YOUR CREDIT

CARD TO FINANCE YOUR PROPERTY
INVESTMENTS !!

What happens if something goes wrong with your
investment as well as you end up paying that 18%
passion on that particular $20,000 for years to
find? Do you want me to do the mathematics on
that?

So, if you're a renter and do not have any home
equity and also you do not have any financial
savings, the only alternative left on our listing to
get going is finding a partner. Finding a partner
will be next to impossible if your very own funds
are ugly. If you have no experience investing in
real estate, you are deep in debt, and you are
trying to get rich on someone else's money,
exactly what remains in it for them, as your
potential partner? It just appears high-risk to me.

If you were to approach me with a financial
investment possibility as well as you said " I have
actually found this home that I believe is an
excellent investment. I don't have any type of
money since when I graduated from college two
years ago, I had $30,000 in pupil finances. I just
have actually $5,000 entrusted to settle. However,
I actually intend to begin property investing as
well as I think this deal will certainly be fantastic,"

I, directly, would certainly be extra curious about dealing with you.

See what I am stating? He or she has no cash. However, they have the ideal mindset of cash. They owe money for a good factor AND ALSO have been diligent concerning debt repayment.

So, if you intend to come to be an investor, however your up to your ears in the red and have an unfavourable total asset, get focused on repairing your cash mess at the same time as you begin learning more about realty. By the time you have a better grip on your money, you can be educated and ready to make your initial purchase also!

The Hidden Keys to Funding Particular Homes in Realty Investing

In numerous areas of the nation, designers purchased tracks of rural land as well as established these right into brand-new residence subdivisions. New homes emerged throughout the landscape and were sold with financing from conventional lending institutions. All in all, these projects succeeded if done pre-2007. Jobs after this time period were usually fueled by barricade capitalist supposition and also several residences were finished yet big portions of these were never ever inhabited or inhabited for a couple of years as the market dropped and these homeowners abandoned their residences.

States like Florida as well as Arizona had huge areas of abandoned houses populate the horizon in some backwoods that were planned to be self-contained suburbs of significant cities typically called bedroom communities. There exist a chance genuine estate capitalists to deal these residences after repossession has happened or a short sale is finished.

So, if you are an investor reading this, ask on your own why other investors aren't jumping all over these immaculate homes that are slowly rotting due to no purchasers. There are basically two factors. Initially, investors can not discover buyers that wish to live in virtual seclusion in these areas. Second of all, the capacity to have end-buyers finance these residential or commercial properties is very limited, particularly to customers with the tested credit report.

There is an expression in property spending that claims that if the cost is right, a person will buy it. This is true, especially if the advertising and marketing effort shows the property to adequate individuals. Advertising and marketing any type of building is essential to making revenues in realty investing, and this exceeds the common technique of using the Numerous Listing Solution. One of the most powerful investors have the biggest customers checklist and can deal with their buildings in days instead of weeks or months.

The first problem is finding the purchasers and several capitalists overlook international customers due to the fact that they are harder to locate. Nonetheless, they are generally money purchasers, so there is no problem with financing a home or obtaining an evaluation appropriate to a lending institution. Funding is the 2nd issue that is often a problem in making these bargains happen. Conventional loan providers, usually the very same loan providers that funded the initial job, do not want to loan on a residential or commercial property where they currently lost 80% or even more of their initial financial investment. Yet a couple of investors have actually located a trick to getting funding for these properties.

As I discussed initially, a number of these sub-divisions have been constructed in backwoods. Not just rural in the feeling of the way out in the country, yet likewise for zoning objectives. This is the key to funding these stubborn buildings. The USDA (USA Department of Agriculture) has financings available for residential properties located in assigned backwoods. Initially created for farmers, these lendings can be made use of by any individual who qualifies as well as where the funded property is in an assigned rural area. Presently, and also this is subject to transform, the credit score need is a 640 FICO rating, and they will certainly finance 100% of the acquisition cost.

In summary, if you are looking to buy distressed homes where developers have fallen short, be careful that you can re-sell them by developing a buyers list in advance as well as seek to lend institutions who will finance in these locations. Retired individuals are exceptional prospects for these jobs as they are living in their houses and also are not commuting to work - so there is usually somebody in the neighbourhood to watch out for criminal damage. The factor these homes are so eye-catching is that they are offering literally at 10% to 20% of the original funded amount as well below the substitute cost of a similar residential property located in a "typical" area. Numerous capitalists are finding these communities are an excellent new source of rewarding deals.

WAYS TO INVEST IN REAL ESTATE IN 2020

In the past 50 years, real estate investing has become increasingly common. Investing property, though, isn't all about discovering the right spot you can call home. This goes beyond advice that can be followed and acted out. Within this segment, authors will introduce you to real estate as an asset and the many ways you can make real estate investment:

Rental - You buy the land, and rent it to a tenant. As the owner, in order to manage the house, it is your duty to cover the taxes, mortgage and other things that need to be undertaken. The owner will set his rental rate to a sum that would be adequate to meet all maintenance costs. Often, landlords can charge more to get monthly income. Ideally; indeed, the safest option will be to be vigilant at reduced cost and bill residents-only enough to offset all expenditures. When the debt is paid off, now is the period for you to receive more of the loan as a fee.

Real estate investment groups -- If you don't want to become a landlord, but you're interested in owning a rental house, investment companies can be ideal with you. A company will buy or construct residential units, and then look through the company for investors to buy units. The company takes over all unit maintenance, including tenant scouting, advertising, and the like. Investment groups regular edition shows the collection under the name of the participant. In this kind of arrangement, in return for running the building or portion, the client takes a percentage of the monthly rent.

Real estate trading - Commonly known as "keep and purchase," traders buy and retain assets for a certain amount of time, then sell the property as the demand is starting to demonstrate positive value. Flipping property can be a really profit-making company. It is a short-term cash gamble, but when a flipper struggles to unload his properties, it can become quite catastrophic.

Simple Ways To Invest In Real Estate

Purchasing a real estate is about having more than just a spot to call home. Throughout the past 50 years, investing in real estate has been extremely commonplace, and is now a growing investment tool. Although the real estate market has plenty of opportunities to make big gains, it is much more complicated to buy and own real estate than to invest in stocks and bonds. We will go beyond purchasing a home in this segment and introduce you to real estate as an investment.

1. Basic Rental Property

This is an undertaking as ancient as the land-ownership tradition. One individual is going to buy a property and rent it to a client. The proprietor, or owner, is liable for paying the property's interest, fees, and upkeep expenses. Ideally, the owner pays adequate rent to offset all of the above expenses. A landlord can even charge extra to produce a monthly income, but the most popular approach is to remain conservative and simply charge enough rent to meet the costs before the lease is charged, by which stage the remainder of the rent is a benefit. In fact, the house could also have increased in value during the mortgage era, providing the lender with a more valued commodity.

2. Real Estate Investment Group

Real estate finance companies are sort of like tiny institutional loan funds. If you are involved in buying a rental property but don't want the bother of becoming a homeowner, a real estate investment company might be the option. A company will buy or construct a set of apartments or condos, and then allow investors to purchase them through the company (thus joining the group). A single owner may control one or more units, but all the units are jointly controlled by the organization running the investment party, taking care of upkeep, advertising empty units and interviewing tenants. The business receives a share of the annual income, in return for this land maintenance.

3. Real Estate Trading

And this is the wild side of investing in real estate. Much like the day traders that are leagues removed from a buy-and-hold buyer, the real estate traders are a totally separate species from the buy-and-rent tenants. Real estate dealers purchase property for a brief period of time (often no longer than three to four months) and market them for a profit. Often called flipping properties, this strategy is focused on purchasing assets that are either substantially undervalued or in a very competitive market.

4. Real Estate Investment Trust

Real estate has been here since our cave-dwelling ancestors started driving foreigners out of their rooms, so it's no wonder that Wall Street has found a way to transform the land into a widely traded tool. A real estate investment trust (REIT) is formed when a company (or trust) uses the money of creditors to purchase and manage income assets. Like like every other property, REITs are purchased and sold on the main exchanges. A business needs to shell out 90 per cent of its gross income in the form of distributions in order to retain its position as a REIT. Through doing so, REITs stop charging corporate income tax, whereas a typical corporation will be taxed on their earnings and would have to consider whether or not to share their after-tax profits as dividends.

5. Leverage

Investing in real estate, with the exception of REITs, offers an owner one option which is not open to capital market investors: leverage. When you plan to buy a product, the entire amount of the product will be charged at the moment you put the buying order. Even if you buy on the margin, the amount that you can borrow is still much smaller than with real estate. Many traditional mortgages need down by 20 per cent. Based on where you stay, though, there are several forms of mortgages needing as little as 5%. This ensures you will manage the whole property and the wealth that it retains by charging just a percentage of the actual valuation. Your mortgage will likely pay the house 's total value at the time you bought it, but you control it the minute papers are signed.

We also looked at increasing forms of assets in real estate. We have just scratched the surface, however, as you may have expected. There are numerous types of real estate assets inside these cases. There is a lot of upside for real estate like for any property, but that doesn't mean that it's a guaranteed benefit. Take deliberate decisions, as in any project, and evaluate the risks and rewards of your acts before jumping in.

Ways To Invest In Real Estate In 2020

You want to invest, and almost all of your wealth is in the equity market at this stage. You know diversification is important, but you're not sure whether investing in real estate is right for you.

You may find that it takes a lot of investment upfront, or it involves a lot of continuing research.

And while some of this is accurate, this year there are different opportunities that can render real estate a great investment for you.

Although investing in immovable property is obviously not for all, it can be very valuable. Many people have made millions into real estate investments. When you choose to expand your financial horizons, here are numerous ways to invest in real estate.

Invest In A Bigger Real Estate Deal

One of our main real estate investment opportunities is joining hands with others to participate in a bigger offer. That may be industrial or residential.

There are two fantastic items on investing in a bigger online real estate deal:

- Small minimums – depending on the program you 're utilizing, you can spend as low as $500 to be a landowner.

- You don't have to be an approved investor – in the past, you used to be an accredited investor to engage in certain kinds of investments, but the law went away with other forms of investments.

- When you're trying to diversify your finances but don't have a ton of capital to do about it, this might be a profitable way to get going.

We suggested two real estate investment platforms:

- **RealtyMogul** – RealtyMogul provides a variety of assets for buyers to select from, including industrial, mixed-use, business and shopping. We do not charge commissions to their creditors, but we place the responsibility on the property holders. Just a few weeks after the project is funded, investors can start seeing a return. We are RealtyMogul partners and believe it's among the best platforms out there right now.

- **Fundrise** – Fundrise is one of the most popular real estate investment sites, with a minimum investment of $500 and fees ranging from 0-3 per cent. The platform is selective in which initiatives it approves-accepting just about 5 per cent of the proposals. Fundrise is another of our favourite sites simply because of the spectrum of property investments they have to choose from, but also because you don't have to be an accredited investor to invest – they 're one of the only platforms that currently allow this.

Buy A Rental Property

Buying and renting houses is a smart means of producing additional monthly cash flow.

To do so, you have to purchase a house with a combined annual interest premium, home insurance premium and lower-income tax bill than the land commands rent. There are several ways to do this-from buying in a high-rent area to putting down a lot of money, so your mortgage payment is low.

You can easily buy rental properties for a single-family (which already have tenants and cash flow) online. There are two downsides of explicitly owning a rental home. First, it usually needs a ton of cash upfront – from the down payment to the necessary upkeep. You just ought to decide if it's worth your return on investment.

The second big drawback to immovable properties is the renters. You may need to test tenants before they are permitted to move in. You're always required at one stage or another to hear sad tales, and you'll have to know how to be consistent with tenants. If you're the sort where people will quickly give up, you could be best off having a property management firm supervise your rental assets. Continuous research is expected anyway.

The residential property can be very lucrative, depending on who you are referring about. And, if you do the hard work of locating such secret treasures, you can let a property management firm do the rest, and rent properties can be a source of semi-passive income.

Flipping Houses

Flipping homes may be very dangerous, but highly satisfying too. However, considering that house prices are on the increase again, now is a smart opportunity to continue selling houses. Flipping a house is the amount of buying a house at market value, restoring it, and then selling it for income.

You need to track down some bargain homes to be a good flipper-the less effort you have to do the easier. The perfect flip home will be one which needs only slight cosmetic repairs. You will instead render the house appear aesthetically more beautiful and a market for income.

If you want to swap houses, you have to plan for the risk that the house will not sell easily – or for a lot of income. While flipping homes, you are taking a huge gamble, which is why you have to pay careful attention to the place, requirements and price of the homes. If you have the talent for flipping homes, however, you may consider that this is one of the best investments you've ever made.

Rent A Portion Of Your Existing Home

If you aren't sold on the idea of purchasing a home only to recoup your income slowly, you might first check the waters by renting a section of your house. You have a few choices to make this possible.

Either you should reserve a spare space at home, or you can reserve the basement. When you do have to purchase your first house, and like this concept, you might also own a duplex, stay in one apartment and rent the next one.

The benefits of renting a part of your house are you being tightly monitoring your occupant. It is less probable that if you're in the same home, a neighbour may want to stiff you up for the rent payment. You do have the option to hire a part of your house and have a feel about what it is like to be a landlord without having such a big monetary commitment.

Real Estate Investment Trusts (REIT)

If you think the real estate is a fantastic opportunity, but you don't want to have the hands-on, you may be willing to transfer the real estate to the capital market.

Real Estate Investment Trusts (REIT) are a perfect means of engaging in real estate without directly involving yourself. A REIT is a fund set up to invest in immovable property specialized mortgage securities, shares, and commodities.

A few specific forms of REITs exist; equity, mortgages, and hybrid. An equity REIT invests in houses, a mortgage REIT invests in mortgages, and the combination of the two is a mixture. Typically these three give large returns-essentially you get charged back by the tax that people spend for their mortgages.

When you're pressed for cash, the way to go is definitely to participate in REITs.

American Capital Agency (NASDAQ: AGNC), Annaly (NYSE: NLY), Realty Income (NYSE: O) are some of the most common REITs.

Dave Grandone

HABITS OF SUCCESSFUL REAL ESTATE INVESTORS

O ver the years, I've come across several real estate developers around the country and interacted with them. I've found that those who outstand with what they do have the same behaviours – without exception.

Incredible right?

Such people come from diverse family groups, industries and invest in multiple forms of real estate. Although they also have disagreements, a mutual desire for excellence always unifies them.

Ever question what they are doing to succeed?

Investing in real estate can be daunting – particularly if you're new to the game, it may be challenging to know how to get going, how much to invest and what to look for in a property before you acquire it. It could feel as if you are continually seeing people investing in real estate, selling homes, wholesaling, or running rentals that seem to have all that together, how do they all learn how to function in this field of real estate investment? We realize that while the real estate developers you see today may look like they've got it all together, at one stage, they too had to go through a period of studying and definitely several failures before they got to the level where they are now. We have clear practices of active real estate investors for you to potentially get some details as to how you should continue investing well today in real estate!

It turns out there are best practice principles to be adopted for active real estate developers so you should still obey them. People who follow their investment goals adhere to values which direct them through the highly competitive real estate sector. Developing a good knowledge of the financial principles and markets that are likely to influence your investment is critical. Begin by investing in a specific form of land, surround yourself with a strong support team and remain active in any element of your investment in order to achieve progress and attain your investment objectives.

Joint partnerships, distribution, and property management are only a couple of the areas in which investors will profit from real estate, but in this dynamic environment, it requires a little bit of expertise to be effective. Although some universities provide courses and programs which directly benefit real estate investors, a degree is not automatically a requirement for successful investment in real estate. Whether an individual owns a degree or not, there are growing characteristics that are typically owned by top real estate investors. Below are the ten patterns which are expressed by extremely successful real estate investors.

There is not much in all honesty, which distinguishes a good company from a mediocre one. Most frequently than not, these are the little items that will compensate for the greatest variations. However, there is one factor which has the potential to catapult even new investors into a successful career: behaviours. The day-to-day patterns you build have far more influence than you may think. There are tasks you can do every day if you want to get the best out of your company. They 're not going to ensure results alone, but they're going to go a fair way toward helping you find your path. Here are ten items any investor can do:

1. Make a Plan

Real estate developers must view their real estate operations as a company in order to create short and long term targets to accomplish them. Additionally, a marketing strategy encourages creditors to see the larger picture and tends them retain attention on the targets rather than on the small losses. Investing in real estate can be difficult and challenging, and a good approach can hold investors focused and on the job.

2. Know the Market

Efficient real estate buyers gain a detailed understanding of their chosen market(s). Keeping up to date with current trends, including changes in consumer spending habits, mortgage rates, and unemployment rates, to name a few, allows real estate investors to recognize current conditions and plan ahead. This helps them to anticipate when patterns can shift, generating future opportunities for the investor prepared.

3. Be Honest

Investors of real estate are generally not obligated to follow a certain degree of integrity. Although making the best of this scenario will be straightforward, best active real estate investors uphold strict ethical standards. Because investment in immovable property requires individuals, the credibility of an owner is likely to be wide-ranging. Active real estate buyers realize that justice is safer than seeing what they might get away with.

4. Develop a Niche

Developing a target is crucial for investors to obtain the breadth of expertise that is key to making it effective. Having the chance to build this degree of awareness of a given field is crucial to long-term progress. If a given sector is perfected, the buyer may use the same in-depth strategy to other markets.

5. Encourage Referrals

Referrals generate a significant portion of the business of an immovable investor, so it's essential that investors know how to respect. This involves business partners, associates, clients, renters and anyone who has a business relationship with the investor. Successful investors in real estate pay attention to detail, respond to feedback and suggestions and portray their industry in a constructive and competent manner. This builds a reputation that makes others interested in collaborating with those investors.

6. Stay Educated

As for every company, it is important to keep up-to-date with the rules, legislation, terminology and patterns that shape the foundation for the company of the real estate investor. Investors can fear losing traction not just in their company but also legal consequences if regulations are broken or violated. Productive real estate investors stay informed and adjust to any shifts in legislation or economic patterns.

7. Understand the Risks

Investors on the equity or derivatives exchange are overwhelmed with alerts on the potential dangers involved with the transaction. Nonetheless, real estate investors are more likely to see ads suggesting just the opposite: that making money in real estate is straightforward. Prudent real estate owners consider the dangers – not just in terms of real estate sales, but also the legal ramifications – and change their companies to rising such dangers.

8. Invest in an Accountant

Taxes form a large part of the taxable expenditures of an immovable lender. It can be difficult to grasp new tax legislation and take time off the company at hand. Strong investors in real estate retain the services of a professional, trustworthy accountant to manage the books of the firm. The expenses involved with the accountant can be negligible compared to the savings that a professional can make to the company.

9. Find Help

Understanding the economics of investing in real estate is difficult for those seeking to do it by themselves. Successful real estate investors also owe part of their achievement to others, whether they are a consultant, advisor or buddy of support. Rather than lose time and energy solving a complicated dilemma alone, active real estate owners realize that accepting the experience of certain professionals is worth the potential costs (in terms of capital and ego).

10. Build a Network

A network will offer valuable resources to both fresh and seasoned real estate buyers and build opportunities. A sort of community, composed of a well-chosen leader, mutual associates, customers or non-profit leaders, helps participants to criticize and encourage each other. Because much of the investment in real estate is based on experiential learning, savvy real estate investors understand the importance of networking.

The Bottom Line

Despite abundant advertisements claiming real estate investment is an easy way to make wealth, it is, in fact, a challenging business that requires expertise, planning and focus. Moreover, because the company is about individuals, consumers profit in the long term from working with honesty and having consideration for employees and customers. While making short-lived income may be fairly easy, creating a company that invests in long-term real estate takes talent, commitment, and these ten critical habits.

Focus on those five things, and you'll have the trust and inspiration to make the best of your day. They are all stuff you should continue tomorrow, without delay at all. Even if you simply decide to take action or read an educational article, you are increasing your chances of succeeding. Begin your day with this stuff, and continue them for a month. Your company will thank you at the end of thirty days.

Keeping reliable is never easy, and often even my top backers have lost their energy too. Consistently act successful investors-no excuses. They may lose concentration, motivation or drive, but their power is still to prevail over obstacles.

Then ask yourself:

Dave Grandone

Are you still keen on learning?

Based on the targets?

Can you ever regularly take action?

Offer yourself a slap on the back if you have three consecutive yes. If not, maybe try harder! Defy yourself!

CONCLUSION

How many late-night real estate infomercials have you seen the immovable wizard sipping cocktails on their beachside home's back deck, beckoning you to visit them in luxurious living?

One of the main draws of real estate investing is probably the picture of developers driving luxury automobiles, residing in huge houses and eventually becoming wealthy. And although many real estate developers are accumulating considerable wealth throughout their careers, investing in immovable property is not a fast-growing scheme. Yes, some are making a lot of money in a short time; however, these circumstances are usually the exception, not the rule.

Property investment takes planning, patience and persistence. Don't plan your first year to make a million dollars. Instead, plan to create a company in real estate that will expand consistently year after year, helping you to meet your financial goals — and eventually make your dreams come true. No matter what you may think, it takes hard work to be effective in real estate, as does every other industry. Knowing that there are no solutions to becoming good in real estate is also important — there are no goods or software that can do the job for you either. You have to understand the principles and then incorporate them. Naturally, our goal here is to support you with that.

If you want to go full time or merely spend on the side, for you and your children, real estate will be the road toward a promising financial future.

Adding real estate to your investment portfolio lets you diversify your investments, so you can better handle uncertainty in the economy. You build a stabilizing force inside your assets by distributing the capital through different types of investments, such as stocks, bonds, and real estate. By the time stocks fell, real estate can start rising (or vice versa).

Do Not Go Yet; One Last Thing To Do

If you enjoyed this book or found it useful, I'd be very grateful if you'd post a short review on Amazon. Your support really does make a difference, and I read all the reviews personally so I can get your feedback and make this book even better.

Thanks again for your support!